Augustus Thomas

Twayne's United States Authors Series

David J. Nordloh, Editor

Indiana University, Bloomington

TUSAS 478

AUGUSTUS THOMAS (1857–1934)
Photograph courtesy of the
Southern Historical Collection, Wilson Library,
University of North Carolina, Chapel Hill

Augustus Thomas

By Ronald J. Davis

State University of New York at Plattsburg

Twayne Publishers • *Boston*

Augustus Thomas

Ronald J. Davis

Copyright © 1984 by G. K. Hall & Company
Published by Twayne Publishers
A Division of G. K. Hall & Company
70 Lincoln Street
Boston, Massachusetts 02111

Book Production by Elizabeth Todesco
Book Design by Barbara Anderson

Printed on permanent/durable acid-free
paper and bound in the United States of
America

**Library of Congress Cataloging in
Publication Data**

Davis, Ronald J.
   Augustus Thomas.

   (Twayne's United States authors series; TUSAS 478)
   Bibliography: p.
   Includes index.
   1. Thomas, Augustus, 1857–1934—
Criticism and interpretation.
I. Title. II. Series.
PS3023.D3   1984   812'.52   84-10858
ISBN 0–8057–7419–X

Contents

About the Author

Ronald J. Davis received the B.A. from Mercer University in Macon, Georgia, and the Ph.D. from the University of North Carolina at Chapel Hill. He is currently associate professor at the State University of New York at Plattsburgh with specializations in early American drama, English Romantic poetry, and journalism. He was primarily responsible for developing Plattsburgh State's print-journalism program and is developing specializations in Old English language and literature and the history of the English language.

Preface

Between 1890 and 1912, American drama advanced from imitation and adaptation of foreign plays, crude melodrama, and escapist literature to occasionally well-crafted theme plays, American in subject and technique. Augustus Thomas (1857–1934) was in the vanguard of that evolution. He was a progenitor of the American drama of ideas, author of America's first serious socioeconomic and political plays, and, in the frequency and breadth of his treatment of American themes, characters, and setting, the most "American" playwright before Eugene O'Neill.

Based on firsthand observation, his regional and national plays, such as *Alabama* (1891), *In Mizzoura* (1893), and *Arizona* (Chicago, 1899), photograph American character, dress, manner, and speech in a particular locale in a particular year. Usually, they are topical, often on a national scale. They are thoroughly American, though, not because they photograph setting, character, and period, but because they study the interrelation of temperament and environment and the resulting evolution of character. Besides regional peculiarities, Thomas portrayed what he considered to be peculiarly American characteristics: freedom of individuality, thorough equalitarianism, and a tendency to idealize. Because his regional/national plays and drama other than farce-comedies examine the interaction of setting and character, Thomas's plots, often conventional and appropriate though not always indigenous to a certain region, are usually background for studies of character and period. One of Thomas's chief contributions to American drama is the resulting redefinition of melodrama. Physical action often is replaced with mental or emotional action. The curtains fall at quiet moments, when emotions are suggested, not expressed through action or gesticulation, but through an economy of words.

Before the rise of muckraking literature (usually dated from the January 1903 issue of *McClure's Magazine*), few cries for political and social reform had been heard in American literature. Thomas's *New Blood* (1894) and *The Capitol* (1895) took a stand on contemporary issues, such as the right of labor to strike, tariffs, and the illegality and abuses of trusts. All play elements, including love interests, advance ideas. These Thomas plays prefigured by thirty-odd years other American plays that rethink and offer a restructuring of the country's political and economic foundations, and they preceded by at least ten years the rise of American thematic drama.

Based on scrutiny of the findings of abnormal psychology and psychical research and personal observation, Thomas's *The Witching Hour, The Harvest Moon,* and *As a Man Thinks*—plays about the faculties, characteristics, and processes of the subconscious mind—enlarged the field of American dramatists to include earnest treatment of psychological and paranormal subjects. They helped open the stage for plays of ideas, invited a more intellectual audience to the theater, and prompted a psychic period in the American drama.

The Thomas plays least dated by nineteenth-century attitudes and most entertaining for today's reader are his comedy-farces. American in subject but French in technique, these plays are models of ingenious construction. Quickly developed and unexpected complications are followed by extrication, usually creating further complication. Ironically, from the perspective of American drama history, these are Thomas's least important plays. They entertain, but they entertain only.

Because they are finally minor works, the farce-comedies are discussed only briefly in chapter 5. More extended chapters are given to Thomas's plays on American geography (chapter 3), political and socioeconomic conditions (chapter 4), and the subconscious (chapter 6). Chapter 1 recounts the formative influences on Thomas as a dramatist and traces his career as a playwright; chapter 7 assesses his contributions as an author and theatrical leader to American drama. Chapter 2 details Thomas's concept of the subconscious mind—the inspiration for his plays on the mind and the first systematic and comprehensive theory of playwriting by an American dramatist. Arguments in chapters 2–6 do not apply exclusively to one chapter. Local color, melodrama refinement, and the interplay of temperament and environment, discussed in the chapter on Thomas's regional and national plays, are central also to his plays on politics, economics, and the mind. Drama techniques structured on a theory of the subconscious, discussed in chapter 2 and applied in chapter 5 to the mind-plays, appear in all of Thomas's plays.

Thomas's role in shaping American drama extends far beyond the contributions of his seventy-odd plays, most of which were performed on the New York stage. As president of the Society of American Dramatists (1906–12) and the American Academy of Arts and Letters (1914–16), and art director of the reorganized Charles Frohman Company (1915–16), he was influential in shaping the theatrical policy of his time. Respected by managers and actors for his fairness and familiarity with every aspect of the theater, Thomas was selected to mediate the 1919 Actors Equity strike. As executive manager of the Producing Managers' Association, he was spokesperson from 1922–24 for the organized theater. In this capacity he tried to establish a national theater and promoted the study and performance of drama nationwide. He was largely responsible for the admission into the United States of the Moscow Art Theatre players and fought drama censorship and legislation that banned children from the stage. Recognized as a leading American playwright, a theatrical leader, and a prominent political figure (he was mentioned more than once as a potential candidate for the presidency), Thomas's opinions on the theater and drama had the weight of authority.

Despite Thomas's contributions to American drama and theater history, he, like all American dramatists before Eugene O'Neill, has been neglected by twentieth-century drama scholars. Except for Arthur Hobson Quinn's twenty-seven-page chapter on Thomas and his picture of American life (*A History of the American Drama*, 1936), he is only mentioned in drama histories. No scholarly article exclusively discusses his plays or contributions to American drama, and no biographical or critical-analytical book on Thomas or his plays exists. This disregard in part is due to the inaccessibility of his plays. Only sixteen of them were published, primarily for copyright protection; none is staged today.

A thorough research of Thomas as person and playwright was impossible before 1949, when Professor James O. Bailey procured from Luke and Lisle Colby, the playwright's son and wife, a number of Thomas manuscripts to be housed in the Southern Historical Collection at the University of North Carolina, Chapel Hill. These holdings were supplemented later by additions from Luke, Lisle Colby, and William Elliott, Thomas's grandson. The resulting Augustus Thomas Collection contains one or more versions of nearly all of Thomas's plays (152 versions in all); five scrapbooks of newspaper clippings covering Thomas's dramatic activity for nearly thirty years; about 350 letters from Thomas to Luke during his son's college years (1910–14); as well as other scrapbooks and correspondence, speeches, sketches, Lisle Colby's unpublished autobiography, even a film of Thomas talking to actor Francis Wilson.

Newspaper reviews (more than a hundred for *Alabama* alone) record critical reaction to Thomas's plays and Thomas's commentary on his plays. His letters to his son offer a workshop view of his composition of plays from 1910 to 1914 and detail the plays the family attended and their critical responses, as well as his theatrical and political activities—his attempts to prevent legislation banning children from the stage, his February 1912 testimony before a congressional committee considering copyright laws, and his March 1913 meeting with President Woodrow Wilson concerning an ambassadorship to be offered to the playwright. His speeches exhibit his thought about political and socioeconomic issues, subconscious-mind processes, and drama and its techniques. Besides supplying material necessary for the study of Thomas, his plays, and his role in the theater, the collection also provides an overview of the forces retarding and advancing the 1891–1911 evolution of American drama.

My gratitude is extended to Professor James O. Bailey, whose informed and generous counsel prompted this study of Augustus Thomas and guided its early stages before his death in 1979; to Professor Mark Reed of the University of North Carolina for his encouragement of my scholarship; and to the staffs of the University of North Carolina, Chapel Hill, Wilson Library; New York Public Library; and State University of New York, Plattsburgh, Feinberg Library. My special thanks is given to Richard A. Schrader and his Southern Historical Collection staff at Wilson Library for their liberal and always friendly assistance. I also thank Professor David J. Nordloh of Indiana University for his scrutiny of the manuscript and helpful suggestions.

Ronald J. Davis

State University of New York at Plattsburgh

Chronology

1857   Augustus Thomas born, January 8, in St. Louis.

1868   Serves as page in Missouri Assembly.

1870–1871   Serves as page in United States Congress.

1871–1877   Railroad employment.

1882   One-act play *The Big Rise* performed in St. Louis.

1883   Organizes Dickson Sketch Club. One-act plays— *Editha's Burglar, A New Year's Call, A Man of the World, A Leaf from the Woods,* and *A Studio Picture*—performed in St. Louis.

1884–1885   Second Dickson Sketch Club tour; *Combustion* performed.

1885–1888   Works as reporter for St. Louis *Post-Dispatch* and Missouri *Republican;* editor and half-owner of the Kansas City *Mirror.*

1889   *The Burglar,* first play to be produced in New York; *A Man of the World* also produced in New York.

1890   Offered position of reviser and adapter of foreign plays by A. M. Palmer.

1890   August 16, marries his childhood sweetheart, Lisle Colby. *Reckless Temple* excoriated by critics for its social criticism.

1891   *Alabama,* first major hit.

1893   *In Mizzoura.*

1894   *New Blood,* first serious socioeconomic play in American drama. A success in Chicago, a failure in New York.

1895   *The Capitol,* first serious political play by an American dramatist, a failure.

1899   *Arizona.*

1901   *On the Quiet.*

1902   *Colorado; The Earl of Pawtucket.*

1902–1905   Residency in Paris.

1903   *The Other Girl.*

1905   *Mrs. Leffingwell's Boots.*

1906–1912   President of the Society of American Dramatists.

1907   *The Witching Hour.*

1909   *The Harvest Moon.*

1911   *As a Man Thinks.*

1912   *The Model; Mere Man.*

1914   Receives the American Academy of Arts and Letters' gold medal for his life work in drama; honorary degree (M.A.) from Williams College.

1914–1916   President of the American Academy of Arts and Letters.

1915–1916   Art director of the reorganized Charles Frohman Company.

1916   *Rio Grande.*

1918   *The Copperhead.*

1919   *The Cricket of Palmy Days.* Mediates the Actors Equity strike.

1921   Honorary degree (D. Litt.) from Columbia University.

1922–1924   Executive chairman of Producing Managers' Association. Tries to establish a National Theater.

1923   Honorary degree (M.A.) from the University of Missouri.

1925   Suffers a stroke.

1926   Failure of *Still Waters* and substantial financial losses.

1934   August 12, dies near Nyack, New York.

Chapter One

Career and Life

Apprenticeship for the American Stage

The seeds of Augustus Thomas's love of the theater and the subject matter of all but one of his thirty-five original full-length plays—his scrutiny of American history, people, locale, and themes—were planted in his youth.

Born in 1857 in St. Louis, Missouri, Thomas grew up in a family Catholic in perspective and national in outlook. Thomas Jefferson, Daniel Webster, and Ulysses S. Grant were household names, and a letter about politics from Abraham Lincoln was a prized family possession. Slavery, the Civil War, and other historical events were burning issues of everyday family conversation.

Thomas's father, Elihu Baldwin (1827–1910), who was instrumental in the formation of the St. Louis Republican party, was active in local politics and in national politics on a local level. He was also involved in national military events. As a volunteer during the Mexican War (1846–48), he served as aide-de-camp to General Zachary Taylor, soon to be the country's twelfth president (1849–50); and in 1861 he made a record run from St. Louis to Jefferson City with forty-nine other armed patriots to prevent the Missouri Assembly from seceding from the Union. During the Civil War he raised a company of Union volunteers and served in the Missouri Assembly before assisting in reopening New Orleans' St. Charles Theatre for the entertainment of occupying Union troops. An occasional actor, he brought home from New Orleans a box of celebrity photographs and anecdotes about actors, and later he regularly attended St. Louis theaters with his son Augustus.

Augustus Thomas's maternal grandmother, Sarah Wilson Garretson—who, as a minor consular official's wife, had managed to be presented to Queen Victoria—exerted the most decisive vocal influence in the family. She gauged Thomas's diction by that of Daniel Webster and Andrew Jackson, both of whom she had heard speak, and held up as standards for Thomas to emulate the likes of Lincoln, the actors Edwin Forrest and Charlotte Cushman, and the archbishop of Cincinnati.

In the winter of 1868, Thomas was one of five pages in the Missouri House of Representatives, and from December 1870 until July 1871 he was a congressional page in Washington. There he regularly attended the theater with his uncle Augustus Wallace Scharit, who evaluated each performance for the boy and introduced him to E. L. Davenport, James Murdoch, and other actors at his dinner table. Thomas shared theatrical lessons with Scharit's son and wrote for the family playhouse his first play, a condensation of Dion Boucicault's *Rip Van Winkle*. He also composed dialogue for the principal conflicts in Sir Walter Scott's *The Lady of the Lake*.

His entire page salary was sent to his family, which was suffering from the father's unwise investments. Thomas provided for his personal needs while in Washington from tips he received as a guide to points of interest in the Capitol, as a procurer of autographs of visitors' favorite statesmen, and as a solicitor for congressmen of copies of their colleagues' printed speeches. To help support his family when he returned to St. Louis in 1871, Thomas, who had ended his consecutive schooling at the age of ten, gave up even irregular school attendance at the age of thirteen. From the winter of 1871 to 1878, when he was twenty-one, Thomas worked for three St. Louis railroads, principally as a clerk on the freight platforms and in the freight yard. Here he developed a sympathy for the platform men, engineers, switchmen, and firefighters, who were not protected by air brakes or other not yet invented safety devices. Witnessing the injury of about one man a month and the attempt by the railroad to get the injured to sign waivers for damages or to settle for surgical and hospital fees, Thomas aligned himself with the workers in what seemed to be a life-or-death struggle.

Though two years younger than the minimum qualifying age of twenty-one, he became a member of the Knights of Labor. Because of his understanding of parliamentary procedure, he was chosen as the master workman of Missouri Assembly

No. 9, presiding over about two hundred workmen during a protracted local strike in 1877. In this year, when railroad strikes were becoming national in scope, Thomas, though underaged, ran on the St. Louis Labor Reform party ticket as a candidate for circuit-court clerk, backed by the Knights of Labor.

Delivering his farewell address to the local assembly in 1878, Thomas exchanged the railroad yard for the law office of John Colby, his future father-in-law and a patron of the St. Louis Sketch Club, to which Thomas belonged. In the summer of 1881, he left the study of law to accept a box-office position at Pope's Theatre in St. Louis and to follow his lifelong love of the theater. His behind-the-curtain education in the theater, however, had begun earlier. Before entering Colby's law office, Thomas had been stage manager for the amateur McCullough Club, for which he rehearsed and directed five plays each season and also acted in several leading roles. After returning from Washington in 1871, Thomas became an amateur actor for the Marion Place Dramatic Club, for which he was to write in 1875 his first full-length play, *Alone.* The organization soon became almost semiprofessional, playing benefits for the Railroad Conductors Brotherhood at the railway division headquarters. Thomas also occasionally filled in professionally as an actor for traveling companies, which were undermining local stock companies. After the cessation of resident stock in St. Louis, he played the juvenile lead once or twice a season when Louisville or other close-by cities were without scheduled performances by traveling companies.

Thomas's liberal behind-the-scenes education continued at Pope's Theatre. While overseeing the distribution of advertisements of upcoming performances, distributing mail for visiting companies, and performing other duties as an assistant treasurer, he formed numerous acquaintances with actors, playwrights, and managers, later valuable to him as a playwright in New York. He also pursued his perennial interest in art, evident in many of his plays and in his sketches in *The Print of My Remembrance* (1922), his autobiography. After returning from Washington, Thomas helped organize the St. Louis Sketch Club and attended a night art class at Washington University, but had to reject a scholarship to study art in Paris, then the mecca for American painters, for the same reason he had declined an appointment to West Point three years earlier. The Thomas family needed his financial support. So his father, in his fifties, could attend medical school, Thomas, during his idle hours at Colby's law office beginning in July 1880 and later in Pope's box office, produced political wood engravings for newspaper illustrations.

In 1883, when Elihu Thomas graduated from the St. Louis Homeopathic Medical College of Missouri, Augustus Thomas joined the Vokes Company, which was to tour the country that summer with a farce, *In Camp*. Thomas met the company in Buffalo, but left it in Chicago to organize a theatrical company, the Dickson Sketch Club, while he completed his last season in Pope's box office. Besides his two-act *Combustion* (1884),[1] several one-act plays were produced at Pope's Theatre during his tenure there: the now-missing *The Big Rise* (1882), probably about the March 1882 Mississippi River floods that left 85,000 persons homeless; *Editha's Burglar* (1883); *A New Year's Call* (1883); *A Man of the World* (1883); *A Leaf from the Woods* (1883); and *A Studio Picture* (1883).

In May of 1884, the Sketch Club, including members from the McCullough Club and Pope's Theatre, began a trial run in several Midwestern states. The regular playbill consisted of two plays coauthored by Thomas and Edgar Smith: *Editha's Burglar,* which had been freely adapted from Frances Hodgson Burnett's story of the same name; and the farce *Combustion.* To Burnett's story of a burglar confronted by a charming eight-year-old girl who offers him her toys to steal instead of the family silverware, Thomas and Smith added sentimental interest and a more complicated plot. They made the hard-boiled burglar, who had deserted his family and was presumed dead, the child's father, and let him gradually recognize his daughter. *Combustion,* which included a theater dress rehearsal, was a grab bag of burlesque, operatic arias, barbershop harmonies of popular songs, dances, and comical situations such as the carving of a tough fowl at a dinner table.

Though the Sketch Club returned to St. Louis in late June with a scrapbook of favorable notices and offers of return engagements, the company's salary was unpaid, a printer's bill was outstanding, and nearly every company member was tempted by offers from theatrical managers who had seen the

Sketch Club perform. Thomas turned down an offer of one hundred dollars a week from Abraham L. Erlanger (who by the 1890s would control the booking rights for most of the important southern cities) to replace the leading man in *Dagmar;* and the company prepared for a road trip to begin near the end of August.

The second road trip retraced much of the territory of its trial run, as well as southern Canada, Indiana, Ohio, Pennsylvania, and the South. Along with its regular bill of *Editha's Burglar* and *Combustion,* the Sketch Club added to its repertoire Sir William S. Gilbert's *Sweethearts* (1874), William Bayle Bernard's *His Last Legs* (1871), and *Muldoon's Picnic* (1882).

The Sketch Club experienced many of the inconveniences typical for road companies of that time. Men's and women's dressing rooms were often nonexistent or separated by only a curtain. Occasionally the company traveled excessive distances between performances or, when first-class tickets were not available, rode huddled with trainmen in the caboose. Frequently, to cover expenses, actors had to forego the weekly salary of forty-five dollars. In Muscatine, Iowa, a janitor pulled a chair to the middle of the stage to examine an overhead coal-oil lamp at the most dramatic moment of *Editha's Burglar.* In New Orleans, the donkey in *Muldoon's Picnic* backed through a rotten canvas backdrop and disappeared from the stage.

The Sketch Club returned to St. Louis in the summer of 1885, deep in debt, and disbanded. The company's ingenue, Della Fox, who had played the child in *Editha's Burglar,* was to become a national star. Edgar McPhail Smith went to New York, where he became a successful writer of burlesques and librettos; the company's principal comic, Frank David, became a Broadway success; and William G. Smythe went East to become William Collier's first manager and the booking manager for many of Belasco's productions. Thomas stayed in St. Louis.

The financial failure of the Sketch Club's road tours is not surprising. By 1880 most productions were established as New York successes before being sent on tour. Unlike its competition, the Sketch Club had neither a New York endorsement nor a recognized star, and it faced fierce competition from prestigious New York road companies and duplicate road companies. During its one-week New Orleans engagement in a shabby theater, the Sketch Club competed against New York companies from the Madison Square, Union Square, and Wallack theaters. Even prestigious New York companies during the 1884–85 season struggled for financial survival. Charles Frohman, who took the Wallack Theatre Company northwest from New Orleans, had to sacrifice the company's baggage and most of the scenery before borrowing money to bring the company home. He arrived in New York bankrupt, with less than a dollar in his pocket.

Despite the economic losses of the Sketch Club tours, the on-the-road experience was invaluable to Thomas. An understanding of what subject matter and techniques would please ethnically diverse American audiences was crucial to the success of American playwrights in the 1880s and later. Until 1910, when the growing popularity of motion pictures contributed to the decline of road tours, producers usually made much of their profits from road performances of plays established in reputation by New York runs. Plays that managers thought would not appeal to audiences nationwide often went unproduced. Thomas also studied American people and locales and became exposed to the witty dialogue, restraint, and precision of the plays of William Dean Howells published in *Harper's Magazine.* In Talladega, Alabama, he observed a ruined gateway, which later inspired *Alabama* (1891), the first play to establish nationwide Thomas's reputation. In New Orleans, he was encouraged by Charles Frohman to write *Editha's Burglar* as a full-length play for possible New York production.

Out of a job on his return to St. Louis in 1885, Thomas began a newspaper career that lasted until August 1888. Soon he graduated from reporting school-board meetings, chicken shows, and the like for the *Post-Dispatch* to more challenging assignments. During the Great Southwestern Railroad strike in the winter of 1886, he was allowed to attend labor planning meetings because of his previous membership in the Knights of Labor and to write up the projected events before they occurred. As soon as the event was confirmed by telephone, the *Post-Dispatch* circulated its account on the streets. While covering for the New York *World* in 1877 the first Kansas election in which women participated, he accepted a liberal offer to become editor and half-owner of the Kansas City *Mirror* and half-owner of a proposed theater. The theater opened with a scheduled week of repertoire by Edwin Booth, renowned Shakespearean actor and one of the country's top stars, and Lawrence Barrett. Snow fell through the theater's unfinished roof, and the *Mirror* had to be liquidated to pay Booth's guarantee of $24,000. Afterward Thomas became an illustrator for the Kansas City *News,* then the St. Louis *Missouri Republican,* for which he also wrote feature articles.

Reporting honed Thomas's playwriting abilities. He improved his skills in sketching character, composing dialogue, spotting the dramatic in news, and concentrating the reader's attention. The reporter's passion for accuracy in details helped determine his habit of studying in person the interplay between the locale he planned to dramatize and its inhabitants. From his newspaper experience, he culled incidents, character bits, and situations for his plays. While covering the illness of the 1884 Republican presidential nominee, James G. Blaine, at Fort Gibson, Indian Territory, Thomas wrote a story about a farmhand who teaches a younger half-Indian girl to read and anonymously pays her expenses at a seminary, only to be rejected because she wants to marry an educated man like an editor or writer. This newspaper article and Thomas's coverage of the "Jim Cummings" express-train robbery form the backbone of *In Mizzoura* (1893). Another big newspaper story of 1885–86—the celebrated murder of one Englishman by another, who left a trunk containing the murdered man's body as security for his boarding bill— was incidentally used in *The Earl of Pawtucket* (1903). And the one-act *A Man of the World* (1889) was originally written as a newspaper feature. The reporters in the unproduced *Pittsburgh, The Capitol* (1895), *The Member from Ozark* (Detroit, 1910), and *The Other Girl* (1903) are among Thomas's most realistic characterizations.

About the time Thomas accepted an editorial position at the *Missouri Republican,* E. H. Sothern, fresh from a success in David Belasco's *The Highest Bidder,* offered to produce Thomas's four-act expansion of *Editha's Burglar* if Thomas would rewrite the second act so that the star would not be absent from the stage. As much as Thomas had been waiting for a producer for the play since his return from the Dickson Sketch Club tour, he declined to sacrifice what he considered to be its artistic integrity.

In August 1888, Thomas accepted an offer to be business

manager for Julia Marlowe, who was to become a major Shakespearean actress. When he arrived in New York, he had received
as good a theatrical education in St. Louis as he could have
received in any city other than New York. The accomplished
New York stock companies at the Union Square, Madison
Square, and A. M. Palmer's theaters typically visited St. Louis,
as well as Detroit, Chicago, and Pittsburgh, after the New York
run of their hits. Thomas had watched the performance of the
great actors of his day, including Edwin Booth, the elder Sothern, Edmund Kean, and Sarah Bernhardt. When he wrote a
condensation of *Rip Van Winkle* at the age of fourteen, he had
already witnessed two performances of that play by Joseph Jefferson, and he was one of a few who had ever seen Junius Brutus
Booth's performance of *King John.* He had also become acquainted with a number of American playwrights, including
Steele MacKaye and William Gillette.

In his trunk on his first arrival in New York, Thomas had
two long and several one-act plays. Of the full-length plays,
only *The Burglar* (1889), which joins the burglar's past and
future and two love subplots to *Editha's Burglar,* was to be produced. The five-act *Pittsburgh* adds the melodrama of labor to
the established types of Gothic, domestic, and nautical melodramas, grafting a number of violent scenes of the 1877 Pittsburgh
strike to the familiar plot of an heiress abducted by a villain
who tries to force her to marry a man she does not love. *A
Man of the World* (1889) untangles a love triangle by applying
the theory of probabilities. Leaving a prosperous business, the
experienced Captain Bradley travels nine hundred miles to set
up a civil engineering office and give a man he does not know
a job, and to reconcile a husband and wife he does not know
are estranged. The merit of the play lies in its novel treatment
of an old theme, its crisp dialogue, and the well-rounded characterization of Bradley. *A Leaf from the Woods,* set at a flour mill
in a Wisconsin frontier community, is Thomas's first local-color
play. It combines conventional elements of sentimental interest:
an easterner looking for his long-lost brother falls in love with
a rural girl who had married the brother before he was hanged
mistakenly as a horse thief. *A New Year's Call,* in which a man
pretends to be drunk after a quarrel with his fiancée to win
back her affection, is notable because of the appearance of Lisle

Colby in the one New York performance of the play. She was to marry Thomas on August 16, 1890. *A Studio Picture,* about a teacher's discovering that a street-boy model of one of his students is his lost daughter in disguise, shows for the first time Thomas's interest in visual art.

Though Thomas's apprentice plays are often flawed in dialogue, characterization, and construction, he matured quickly as a playwright, as can be seen by a comparison of the Library of Congress and University of Pennsylvania copies of *The Burglar.* The Library of Congress typescript, dated 1885 and thus only slightly later than the University of Pennsylvania version, has less archaic diction, more crisp dialogue, and an absence of long passages spoken by one person. Expletives like "pshaw," "Why, I declare," and "egads" are deleted; and overly melodramatic expressions and gestures are toned down. Thomas's early long-winded rhetorical dialogue was becoming more succinct and pregnant with wit. Realistic and fresh characterizations, such as Captain Bradley in *A Man of the World* and the reporter Hicks in *Pittsburgh,* were standing out among stock characters. Serious concerns such as the socioeconomic theme in *Pittsburgh* occasionally joined the sentiment and spectacle. Derivative as the apprenticeship plays are, they point toward later directions in Thomas's plays. *A Leaf from the Woods* foreshadows Thomas's local-color plays, such as *Alabama* (1891), *In Mizzoura* (1893), and *Arizona* (1899). Its quietness, absence of melodramatic action, and avoidance of a happy ending—the easterner and his brother's widow do not marry—point toward Thomas's refinement of the crude melodrama of his day. *Pittsburgh* anticipates the socioeconomic and political themes of *New Blood* (1894) and *The Capitol* (1895). *A Man of the World* and *A New Year's Call* roughly prefigure Thomas's idea plays, such as *The Witching Hour* (1907) and *As a Man Thinks* (1911). *Combustion* looks forward to his more refined farce-comedies of the early 1900s, such as *On the Quiet* (1901), *The Earl of Pawtucket* (1903), *The Other Girl* (1903), and *Mrs. Leffingwell's Boots* (1905). Most important, all the apprentice plays are American in theme, character, and setting.

Thomas's first trip to New York did not result in the production of any of his apprentice plays. His position as business manager for Julia Marlowe turned out to be that of a ticket

collector, and his manager became dictatorial, so Thomas returned to St. Louis, being engaged on the day of his return as
advance man for American mind reader Washington Irving
Bishop. Thomas preceded Bishop to areas where the telepathist
would perform, generated publicity, and made all the arrangements for his exhibitions. His association with Bishop, termi-
nated by the psychic's death after a New York City performance
on May 12, 1889, had a profound effect on Thomas. He became
a student of psychic and psychological subjects, dramatizing
these matters in a number of his plays, including the highly
successful *The Witching Hour* and *As a Man Thinks,* early American theme plays.

New York Dramatist

Regional and Political Plays, 1889–99.   In the early summer of 1889, Thomas, in New York, accepted an offer to have
The Burglar produced. He could have made a small fortune
from the play, but dissatisfied with the $40 a week called for
in his contract, he sold the rights for $2,500. The success of
The Burglar, which played in New York and on the road for
the next ten years, and *A Man of the World* (1889) spurred
manager A. M. Palmer to sign Thomas in the spring of 1890
to Dion Boucicault's previous position of reviser and adapter
of foreign plays. Thomas's first play for Palmer, the one-act *A
Woman of the World* (1890), was not convincing in its characterization of a woman who saves her husband's firm after learning
her thoughtless expenditures are about to bankrupt the company. His next play, *Reckless Temple* (1890), was an even more
conspicuous failure. This society drama and psychological study
of compulsive behavior concerns a locomotive engineer whose
feeling of guilt for not protecting his sister, who died giving
birth to an illegitimate child, leads to murder and attempted
murder. Thomas's first firm exploration of a psychological subject in a play was above the heads of the audience and the
critics. The attack in the play on social conventions and snobbery
was not. Critics were offended by the Bohemian character of
the hero and the criticisms of the snobbery and shallowness
of polite society. Thomas's natural bent to produce plays making
serious statements, consequently, was impeded: only in *New*

Blood (1894) does he again openly criticize the social fabric. His tarnished reputation as a dramatist was only slightly enhanced by the favorable reception of his one-act play for actress Agnes Booth, *Afterthoughts* (1890), which depicts an older woman persuading a younger man she loves to return to a younger woman who also loves him.

Physically run-down during the production of *Reckless Temple,* Thomas, turning in early one night, saw against his closed eyelids the ruined gateway he had viewed in Talladega during the second Dickson Sketch Club tour. Then a scene repeated itself: an old man walked through the gateway and stood momentarily before being joined by a young girl; she took him by the hand and led him out of the picture. A day or two later, Thomas had written a one-act sketch of their relationship, which he lengthened to a four-act play by January 1891 and presented to Palmer as *Alabama.*

Exhibiting a lack of confidence in a native product common among American managers, Palmer rehearsed *Alabama* three times, only to withdraw it each time in favor of an English play. After the three English plays had failed and Palmer had not renewed Thomas's contract, *Alabama,* without promotion and in a spirit of desperation, was produced on April 1, 1891. The next morning, Thomas, on a train to Chicago as press agent for a touring English actor, found himself famous.

The play was nearly unanimously reviewed as marking a new development in American drama. Its theme—the need for the regeneration and reintegration of the South into the national life through northern capital, investment, and industry—is thoroughly American, as are the characters and setting. Among the American character types are the unreconstructed southerner, who hates the North for having "robbed" him "of everything that made life worth living"; the new southerner, his son, who wants to invigorate the South without destroying its traditions; the chivalrous southern gentleman; and the greedy southerner, indifferent to southern ideals and honor. The setting for the play is the romantic, idealized, idyllic South, not the South shattered by the Civil War; and in contrast to the violence in *Reckless Temple, Pittsburgh,* and *The Burglar,* the melodrama is quiet in atmosphere.

Alabama was an unqualified success. It was also a turning

point in Thomas's career. Palmer signed him to another one-year contract, and the actor Nat Goodwin, famous for his light comedy and burlesque, paid him an advance of $2,500 to write a serious play. Ironically, the triumph of *Alabama,* the proceeds from which built him a home in New Rochelle, New York, partially slowed Thomas's development as a playwright. After his adaptation from German of Von Moser's *The Woman Who Has Been to Paris* (1891) and his collaboration on *For Money* (1891), a comic character sketch of businessman Winfield Farragut Gurney, Thomas wrote two plays that were not inspirations, but attempts to capitalize on the popularity of southern stories, heightened by the success of *Alabama. Colonel Carter of Cartersville* (1892), an adaptation of Francis Hopkinson Smith's best-selling novelette of the same name (1891), is basically a composite character sketch of an antebellum southerner—the gentleman of chivalry, hospitality, and lofty ideals charmingly adrift in the 1890s, unaware of contemporary business practices. *Surrender* (1892), produced melodramatically by Charles Frohman, is an untraditional Civil War play treating the North and South even-handedly and their conflict comically.

The year 1893 saw the production of Thomas's second major regional play, *In Mizzoura,* and the one-act *A Proper Impropriety,* based on the coincidence of two strangers recognizing in each other a resemblance to a former or current acquaintance. *In Mizzoura,* like *Alabama,* was praised as an American play. Though its characters are romanticized, the depiction of the quiet, kindhearted sheriff was a departure from the stage character with his conspicuous bravery and blazing guns. The setting in nearly frontier-like Pike County in 1891—with rough mud roads, partially broken-down rail fences, and the primitively furnished home of the blacksmith—is realistic, as are the villagers' vulgate provincialisms.

Between 1893 and the production of *Arizona,* his next major regional play, in 1899, Thomas was busy, writing nine full-length plays and three one-act playlets; but none was a box-office or critical success. *The Poor Girls* (1894), adapted from the German, portrays representatives of capital and labor, counterbalancing their virtues and flaws, in a melodramatic plot set in England. The relative success of the play may have influenced the managerial decision to stage *New Blood* (1894), the first

American play seriously to criticize the capitalistic system and offer a solution to the capital-labor conflict. *New Blood* dramatizes the struggle between outmoded ideas favoring trusts, represented by an aged capitalist, and new blood, represented by his son, who prevents the formation of a farm-equipment trust and survives an attempt by the would-be trust members to bankrupt the company he manages. The play had a fine run in Chicago, where the Pullman strike was raging and the play seemed written for the occasion, but not in New York, where the audiences were politically more conservative. Like *New Blood, The Capitol* (1895) is a milestone in the history of American drama. Political corruption in plays before 1895 had been presented only farcically or satirically. *The Capitol,* criticizing the influence of industry and religion on Congress, is the first American drama to study seriously the roots of congressional corruption. Critics and audiences alike were not ready for the staging of modern issues; the play was a dismal failure. Thomas did not again make a serious political or socioeconomic issue central to a full-length play until 1926 in *Still Waters,* an anti-Prohibition play.

After the failure of his political and socioeconomic efforts, Thomas returned to the regional play in *The Hoosier Doctor* (1898), a quiet realistic comedy of the domestic life of good people of meager means in a small Indiana town, and wrote a historical play of colonial times in *Colonel George of Mount Vernon* (1898), primarily a vehicle for exhibiting George Washington's sterling qualities. His *The Meddler,* a contemporary comedy of errors with an ingeniously well-developed string of complications, best deserves the label of forerunner to Thomas's successful farces of the early 1900s. Three playlets—*The Music Box* (1894), *The Man Upstairs* (1895), and *That Overcoat* (1898)—were also produced in the period between *Alabama* and *Arizona,* as well as three full-length adaptations: *Chimmie Fadden* (1896), from E. W. Townsend's series of dialect stories of the Bowery; *The Jucklins* (1897), from the best-selling Opie Reed novel of the same name; and *The Bonnie Brier Bush* (1897), a revision of James MacArthur's dramatization of a novel by Ian Maclaren.

Feeling written out and dissatisfied with the inventions and rewrites he had authored to make a living after the failures of *New Blood* and *The Capitol,* Thomas now resolved to turn to a plain and primitive American subject. On March 17, 1897, he

arrived at Fort Grant, Arizona, looking for a play, but with
no preconceived notion as to story. At the army post and from
visits to a nearby ranch and an outpost, where he saw Apaches
at firsthand, Thomas absorbed local color, found models for
characters, and began developing a plot. Back in New York,
he heard the *Maine* had sunk in the Havana harbor and replaced
the Indians in his first draft with the gathering of cowboys to
fight in the Cuban war.

With the outbreak of the Spanish-American War in April
1898, theater managers became cautious in staging new productions. With no prospect of production for his melodrama of
the Southwest, Thomas made his first trip abroad (June–August
1898). In England he met the playwrights George Bernard Shaw
and James M. Barrie and the satirist Max Beerbohm; in Paris
he heard the socialist Jean Jaurès speak. After Thomas returned
home, *Arizona* opened in Chicago in the summer of 1889. The
play, which captures the atmosphere of military life on the alkali
plains of Arizona and creates several memorable characters, was
an instantaneous and sustained hit. It grossed more than any
other play until then produced in America, with royalties
amounting to a quarter of a million dollars for the first five
years of its performance.[2]

When Charles Frohman, regretting his failure to produce *Arizona,* ordered another regional play, Thomas traveled to Colorado for a story about the mines there. He posed as a mine
owner seeking new investments, helped dig an assessment, en-
countered claim jumpers, and descended eight hundred feet
in a four-foot-square shaft to inspect a gold mine. In the resulting
Colorado (1901), the dirty little Irish miner and the Cornishman
(called Jack as are all Cornishmen in the Colorado mines) came
from Thomas's observation, as did the string of burros pulling
ore cars up a mountain trail and the three different pronuncia-
tions of the word *Colorado.* The play, encumbered with too
many plot threads and too much love interest, was a commercial failure. Two other local-color plays, also produced during
Thomas's period of farce-comedies (1899–1906), are closest
in kinship to his regional plays. *The Soldiers of Fortune* (1902),
a fairly faithful adaptation of Richard Harding Davis's novel
of the same name, presents a conspiracy to overthrow a president
and set up a dictatorship in the fictitious and exotic South Ameri-

can Republic of Valencia. It includes two thoroughly American types: a pioneer of developing countries who has built railroads in the wilderness and wrestled from the earth mountains of iron, and a Gibson girl of the 1890s. *The Ranger* (1907), originally a serious play with a political theme, was revised to suit Charles Frohman into a melodrama with United States Rangers chasing criminal miners and fighting off an attack by Mexicans in a small town on the Mexican frontier. The play was a decided box-office failure, with Frohman losing nearly thirty thousand dollars on it.

Farce Comedies, 1900–1906. From 1900 and the production of *Oliver Goldsmith* through 1906, Thomas entered his second major dramatic phase: frequently discarding his earlier regional local color and melodrama, he chiefly wrote comedies verging on farce. The later of these comedies—American in subject and characterization, but French in technique—are indebted to Thomas's residency in Paris from 1902–5.

Oliver Goldsmith is Thomas's only original play not American in subject matter. The Georgian atmosphere in this situation comedy is convincingly re-created, but remains in the background, as Thomas focuses on the characterization and wit of members of the Johnson literary circle and the principal theatrical event in Goldsmith's life. In act 1 Goldsmith mistakes a country house for an inn, and his friends, gathered there, help foster this misimpression. At the end of the act, Goldsmith determines to use this joke as the plot of a play, *She Stoops to Conquer.*

After *Oliver Goldsmith*, Thomas primarily constructed his farce-comedies by using a formula of complication, followed by extrication, followed by further complication. In act 1 of *On the Quiet*, Thomas figuratively gets his hero up a tree by having him agree not to see the woman he is in love with during his college years. In the second act, the playwright throws stones at his hero by having the girlfriend arrive at his New Haven quarters as he is giving a breakfast for, among others, two music-hall girls. And in the third act, the playwright extricates the hero from the knotty situation. The fast pace, witty, brisk dialogue, and inventive construction of complications with unexpected situations are characteristic of all Thomas's farce-comedies. *On the Quiet* was successful, as were Thomas's next three farce-comedies—*The Earl of Pawtucket, The Other Girl,* and *Mrs.*

Leffingwell's Boots—all running for more than 120 consecutive nights in New York.

In *The Earl of Pawtucket,* Thomas revises the familiar literary motif of an English nobleman in search of a socially ambitious American heiress. In his play, an English earl courts an American divorcée unknowingly assuming her ex-husband's identity. He is forced to pay alimony and is nearly arrested for murder of the missing ex-husband. In *The Other Girl,* capitalizing on American interest in prize fighting after the repeal of the Horton Law, the role of Kid Garvey is modeled on world-champion middleweight boxer Kid McCoy. The characterizations of Garvey, retained to train Reverend Bradford in physical combat, and the athletic minister, whose irrepressible humor prompts him to laugh at funerals and other solemn occasions, were an immediate hit, as was the staging—for the first time in America, Thomas thought—of an ether intoxication. The inspiration for *Mrs. Leffingwell's Boots* was French dramatist Henri Dumay's wager in 1903 that Thomas could not make more than a one-act play out of a dinner party the Thomases had hosted ten years before on the day of a blizzard. Only one guest had arrived—a woman in the arms of her coachman. The standard materials of farce-comedy appear in *Mrs. Leffingwell's Boots:* intrigue, a jealous husband, misunderstandings, type characters, lovers' spats, absurd situations, mistaken identities, and a happy ending. But the play is witty in dialogue, clever in construction, and contemporaneous in allusions.

Thomas wrote four other comedies during his farce-comedy phase: *Champagne Charlie* (1901); *The Education of Mr. Pipp* (1905), a dramatization of cartoons by illustrator Charles Dana Gibson; *DeLancey* (1905), a starring vehicle written for John Drew; and *The Embassy Ball* (1906). *The Education of Mr. Pipp* is the first professionally produced American play constructed from a complete series of pictures. *DeLancey, The Embassy Ball,* and *Champagne Charlie* lack memorable characters, engaging stories, and witty dialogue. Thomas was tiring of the farce-comedy vein.

Psychological and Psychic Theme Plays, 1907–11.   In 1907 Thomas entered his third major dramatic phase—a period of serious theme plays about paranormal cognition, pathological states, and subconscious-mind processes. *The Witching Hour*

(1907), *The Harvest Moon* (1909), and *As a Man Thinks* (1911) were not Thomas's first theme plays, as his contemporaries thought: *New Blood* and *The Capitol* and, to a lesser extent, *Alabama* and parts of *Reckless Temple* give ample evidence of his disposition to write serious plays interpreting important American themes. They are, however, among the first American plays to help establish a drama of ideas on the American stage. The character, action, and settings of *The Witching Hour* develop two themes: the dynamic nature of thought and the accountability of each person for the quality of his thought. During the play a compulsive fear of cat's eyes leads a promising architect to have a dishwater character and to commit an accidental murder; during his trial, public thought telepathically influences a sequestered juror; and hypnotic suggestion disarms a would-be assailant, disgruntled with the jury's verdict of "not guilty." The play is not a typical melodrama of psychic phenomena, for Thomas's play rejects popular notions of paranormal phenomena and is founded on the inquiries of abnormal psychology and psychical research. The powers to read and influence the thoughts of others, living and dead, to immobilize them through suggestion, and mentally to choose one's psychological and pathological sensations are made not unique to a gifted few, but are, according to the play, powers all persons possess to a greater or lesser degree, and influences to which all are susceptible. *The Witching Hour,* the biggest theatrical hit of 1907, helped widen the American stage to include new and serious subject matter.

In *The Harvest Moon,* Thomas continues his study of pathological states, such as hysteria, and the laws of suggestion being developed by abnormal psychology. The effect of eighteen years of negative suggestion on an impressionable girl is dramatized: Dora Fullerton, repeatedly told she has inherited her dead mother's vacillation and waywardness, acts accordingly. She runs away from school, accepts and then breaks an engagement, and against the wishes of her foster parent becomes an actress. Thomas's second major idea play failed to please New York audiences, primarily because a secondary theme of the emotional effect of colors detracted from the main story. *The Matinee Idol* (1909)—a musical comedy in which an improvident actor poses as a hypnotist doctor—capitalizes on public interest in paranormal phenomena. *As a Man Thinks* explores the effect of emotion on an individual's physical and psychological health. A woman suffers from insomnia because of her resentment of the sexual double standard in society, and her husband becomes psychosomatically ill because he doubts the legitimacy of his eight-year-old son. Because of the family tension, the child also becomes ill. In the best dramatization of Thomas's ideas, Dr. Seelig, a wealthy and charitable Jewish physician, unobtrusively expounds the need to cultivate serenity and altruism in thought and deeds, and to forgive discrimination. *The Member of Ozark* (1910), originally written about 1899, is Thomas's only play produced during this dramatic period not to treat paranormal phenomena. In this revised melodrama of political corruption and romance set at the Missouri capital, a new representative defeats a railroad bill devised by a trust as a camouflage for stealing valuable mineral land.

Decline in Reputation as a Dramatist, 1912–34. From 1912 through 1914, the Thomas trademark as a dramatist became tarnished. Of five plays produced during this time, only one, *At Bay* (1913), a melodramatic detective story written with George Scarborough and produced under his name, was successful. *The Model* (1912), which grafts Thomas's view of the elevating nature of the arts onto a potboiler plot in one of his old manuscripts, had too much talk and too many digressions. It ran for only seventeen performances, as did *The Battle Cry* (1914), an adaptation of a Charles Neville Buck novel about feuding Kentucky clans uniting against outsiders, which included twenty-three panoramic "motion picture scenes" with stage voices synchronized with screen action. *Mere Man* (1912), a satirical comedy exploiting various theories on the woman-suffrage question, ran only eight nights; and *Indian Summer* (1913), exploring the role of self-sacrificing heroism, women, and art in uplifting mankind, saw only twenty-four performances. *Three of Hearts,* a collaboration with Martha Morton, was staged in 1915 without mention of Thomas's joint authorship.

In his last six plays, Thomas returned to old forms and themes. *The Soul Machine* (1915) is a melodrama with a psychic villain, a telepathic girl, a doctor who has studied auras for medical diagnosis, and a machine that measures conscious and subconscious emotions by registering the electricity generated by the mind. *Rio Grande* (1916) marks a return to the regional play that had been successful for Thomas in the 1890s. Traveling to military posts along the Rio Grande, he collected local color for a well-developed study of the inner struggle of a colonel and his wife over her infidelity during World War I, when Mexico was threatening raids on the United States. *The Copperhead* (1918) is another local-color play, set in a southern Illinois rural town in 1861, 1863, and about 1900. A supposed Copperhead forty years after the Civil War tells about a midnight meeting in which Abraham Lincoln swore him into secret service as a northern spy. In what reviewers nearly unanimously agreed was one of the great moments in theatrical history, the presence of Lincoln seemed to fill the theater. Another period piece, *The Cricket of Palmy Days* (1919), borrowing from Bret Harte's gold-rush stories, brings to life the days of traveling theatrical companies and the gold rush in the Far West. *The Blue Devil* (1920) is an inferior farce filled with implausible complications; and *Nemesis*—produced in 1921, a year before the publication of Thomas's highly anecdotal autobiography, *The Print of My Remembrance*—is an adultery and murder melodrama wedded to a criminal-justice and psychological play with several instances of Freudian psychoanalysis.

Between 1919 and 1925, Thomas was active in opposing the Eighteenth Amendment, which he thought violated the separation of church and state mandated by the Bill of Rights. To encourage the repeal of Prohibition, he wrote *Still Waters,* a treatise play encyclopedically compiling its wrongs. Unable to find a producer, he invested in the production of the play all his available capital, including his life insurance, and all he could borrow. The play opened in Washington, D.C., with Thomas, now sixty-eight, playing the leading role. In its short run at the capital, *Still Waters* stirred political controversy; but, in its propaganda, cardboard characterization, and meandering plot development, it failed dramatically.

In December 1925, Thomas suffered a stroke, affecting his right side and his speech. By persistently reciting difficult Shakespearean passages, he recovered his speech and delivered a curtain speech when *Still Waters* opened in New York in March 1926. Gradually, his muscle functions, except those of his right hand, returned. Prohibited from playwriting by high blood pressure and irregular heart beats, Thomas patiently developed his left hand by sculpturing five busts; those of Frederic Remington and dramatist William Gillette became part of the Academy of Arts and Letters Collection.

With the 1929 stock market crash, the house built by *Alabama,* Thomas's first dramatic success, now encumbered with unpaid taxes and mortgages, was repossessed. Thomas died of a heart attack August 12, 1934, in the Clarkson Country Club, near Nyack, New York.

Chapter Two

Dramatic Theories
and Techniques

In 1914 Augustus Thomas received the most prestigious award presented an American playwright—the gold medal of the American Academy of Arts and Letters, conferred on the playwright whose life work has improved the craftsmanship of American drama. His mastering of craft had been gradual, but not accidental or limited to a study of dramaturgy. Researching medical and psychological, scientific and pseudoscientific literature, he developed a concept of the subconscious mind of individuals and a collective subconscious that vitally influenced his dramatic techniques and definitions of drama, the theater's services, and the playwright's responsibilities. The dramatist through the conflict in the play stimulates, he thought, the audience's subconscious instincts, arouses its emotions, and stirs it to action. Through personifying all the forces in the play and using character, action, accessories, and setting as symbols, the playwright, according to Thomas, takes advantage of the imagistic language of the subconscious mind, which is affected by suggestion and has a need to have its thought visualized. The play, Thomas believed, should tap the contemporary collective subconscious of America and express nobility, charity, and other racial ideals, embedded in the subconscious. Thus, Thomas defined the good and successful play as articulating an idea deeply felt by the author and the public. The play is developed by conflict in which characters maintain nobility through emotional stress. Because the theater instructs by arousing emotions and gives vicarious expressions to heroic or criminal tendencies in the spectators, the playwright is a moral force in society.

Concept of the Subconscious

Thomas's views of the nature and techniques of drama, inter-
locking like mathematical theorems, are the first systematic and
comprehensive theory of playwriting by an American dramatist.
Behind the theory lies Thomas's concept of the characteristics,
faculties, and powers of the subconscious mind. Whereas the
conscious mind includes the rational, logical, and sensory faculties, the subconscious mind has the powers of intuition, telepathy, and clairvoyance; the faculties of mimesis and instincts;
and several unique characteristics (it is the seat of emotions,
is unable to reason inductively, can be controlled by suggestion,
and expresses itself through images).

All paranormally gained knowledge, Thomas thought, could
be explained by intuition, clairvoyance, and telepathy. Intuition
allows the subconscious mind without learning by the conscious
mind to perceive the higher, altruistic instincts of the human
species. Telepathy, Thomas felt, was pervasive. It entered into
even major business and financial transactions and the events
of everyday life, and would be widely employed in the future
for communication, physical healing, and moral reform. Everyone, he thought, even the spirits of the dead, is capable of
receiving and transmitting telepathic impressions, but women
are more receptive and men more dynamic in the exercise of
this power.   ❉

The telepathically transmitted data, like radio waves, are invis-
ible and able to traverse distance. The strength of the transmission depends on the clarity and definiteness of the thought and
the intensity of the emotion. Thoughts and feelings can also
be telepathically received from another. When two thoughts
appear in an individual's subconscious mind, one being his own
and the other an opposing thought telepathically sent by another,
then the stronger thought will rise to the surface of the conscious
mind.

Dynamic thoughts and feelings are telepathic electrical forces
that contend for dominance and existence within an individual
and between individuals, on a conscious and subconscious level.
Dynamic thoughts and feelings, operating like magnetized wires,
also draw to themselves those waves and currents of sufficient
affinity in the air. Results are achieved for which the individual

does not seem responsible but which are consistent with his desires. The artist's "need of a particular bit of information," for example, is frequently "followed by the seemingly accidental appearance of that information."[1] Many so-called coincidences, Thomas thought, are not accidental. The individual, according to Thomas, is not totally responsible for telepathic phenomena. In speaking of the magnetism of the actor, Thomas said that "its possessor is not its generator but its medium";[2] the generator is a "subtle universal current that sweeps through all mankind, just as the electric current goes through . . . lights."[3] Requisite to becoming an instrument of this cosmic power is an individual's ability to relax and become receptive to its psychic force.

Besides the powers of intuition, telepathy, and clairvoyance, the subconscious mind possesses the faculties of mimesis and the instincts. The stronger mimetic faculty is universal in time, appearing, for example, in the Indians' enacting of the slaying in a buffalo dance and the caveman's recounting to his mate the killing in the forest. It forms the basis of all arts and is responsible for, among other things, verbal communication. Man's survival and progress depend upon this faculty, which stems from the psychological need to respond to externally received sensations and impressions and to express or to see visualized feelings and thoughts.

Possessing the faculty of instincts, as well as that of mimesis, the subconscious mind is also the seat of emotions, an important characteristic, because, as Thomas thought, emotions are responsible for all actions. An emotion is aroused by the stimulation of an instinct or an "attack" on it by an environmental force.[4] Instincts, which are inherited racial habits and not individually acquired traits, are embedded in human consciousness like deposits in stone or strata in the earth. Thomas diagrams these strata of instincts with self-preservation at the base, followed consecutively by the instincts of reproduction, defense of progeny or kin, patriotism, altruism, and awe.

The longer the stratum and the closer it is to the base of the triangle of instincts, the more universal and more deeply embedded, thus less easily eradicated, is that specific instinct. Thus, self-preservation is universal, but the instinct of reproduction less so, and the remaining instincts less still.

The evolution of instincts from animal to man, a progression from self-immersion to selflessness, is not accidental but is due to the attempt by the infinite subconscious mind to express its altruistic nature through the medium of people and events in the sensory world. That man is the strongest, physically and psychically, and most healthy, who becomes the instrument of this expression. Thomas usually designated this harmony with nature's will as heroism and nobility.

Besides faculties, the subconscious mind possesses several important characteristics: its imagistic linguistic medium, inability to reason inductively, amenability to suggestion, and perfect memory. Whereas there can be no constructive thought without words, there are emotions so profound that they cannot be expressed by the verbal language of the conscious mind. These emotions, however, can be suggested by the visual language of the subconscious mind, a language evidenced by the tendency to see images during pathological states, visual illusions in the dark, and dream and hypnagogic imagery.

Images are important in receiving and transmitting telepathic content. Telepathy Thomas defined as a "picture firmly and persistently held in the mind of one man [which] could impress the mind of another and set up similar mental images in that second mind."[5] Images are also important in the affairs of everyday life. Thomas defined an ideal as a "mental picture more or less persistently held in the mind of a person, and more and more insistently governing that person's conduct,"[6] and believed that goals were achieved by holding them as well-defined ideals in the mind. Whereas the direction of an individual's progress depends upon the loftiness or the elevation of the ideal, the rapidity with which he reaches that ideal depends upon his "powers of visualization." Though Thomas believed that men "differ in degree, perhaps in kind, in their capacity mentally to see forms,"[7] he thought that the ability to visualize could be learned and that it was best developed by a disposition to draw.

The subconscious mind's amenability to suggestion makes everyone, at all times, susceptible to suggestion, whether it is direct, as in a physician's oral prognosis, or indirect, as in the environment. Conscious suggestion is mainly constructive, being made by preachers, physicians, and teachers. Unconscious suggestion, for example, the health inquiry and patent medicine advertising, is generally destructive.

Whereas each individual possesses a subconscious mind, each race or nation possesses a collective subconscious mind. Believing in the dynamic power of telepathy and being familiar with the idea, current in his time, that for the subconscious mind distance and space do not exist, Thomas considered individual minds thinking and feeling similarly as creating a public subconscious mind. This collective mind is not an abstraction, a metaphor for a sum of the private minds, but a living and functioning entity. The magnetic wires of individual minds alike in content and purpose create a national magnetic wire, a zeitgeist.

Also related to Thomas's conception of individual and racial subconscious minds is his concept of a cosmic subconscious mind. This force, all-wise and benign like the Christian God, possesses a will; subject, as are humans, to the law of the necessary expression of all adequate impressions, this purposive but unconscious force seeks articulation through the medium of the sensory world. It can communicate with human subconscious minds through the latter's power of intuition and imparts physical and psychic strength, as well as good health, to those individuals who are unselfish and have learned to relax and surrender themselves to its diverse energy. Material events are not accidental, but are symbolic of its woven design. Evolution, for example, especially man's evolution from animals, his development of higher instincts, and his advancement toward civilization, derives from its altruistic goal or ideal.

Thomas's Dramatic Theories and Techniques

On this general concept of the conscious and subconscious minds Thomas based his prescriptive definition of drama. The good and successful play, according to Thomas, articulates an idea firmly in the public mind and deeply felt by the author. It imitates nature, communicates emotion through a story developed by conflict in which characters maintain nobility through emotional stress, and is presented on a stage before an audience.

Behind Thomas's aesthetic theory concerning the dramatist's selection of material for his plays lies his conception of the subconscious mind of the race. To be successful, the playwright needs to "reach the level of current desires,"[8] and in "sensing the mood of the hour" to visualize something in the public mind.[9] Thus the stage does not create, but "seizes and rearranges and presents and makes clear those [ideas] that are being created for it."[10] To Thomas, "no material is useful for a play until it has been used as subject matter for all other literary forms, and made familiar to the public through poetry, fiction, lectures and reportorial comment."[11]

Other literary genres, besides the drama, primarily create and stimulate interest in certain areas of thought. The playwright capitalizes on already existing thought and, in doing so, utilizes a psychological law "that imposes upon us the necessity of seeing our thought put into action."[12] There is, says Thomas, "something in man's constitution that makes the theater necessary."[13]

The drama is more suited than other literary genres for fulfilling this psychological need. It heightens the immediacy of its subject matter by presenting events as occurring in the present. And its subject matter is primarily presented through a visual medium instead of, as in poetry, through descriptive phrasing.

In articulating an idea firmly in the public mind, the play, like all art forms, communicates emotion through an imitation of nature. The communication of emotion through art, like all communication, depends upon a fixed standard that all men can understand and which, by means of the mimetic faculty, they can imitate. A failure to imitate nature, as in cubism and impressionism, according to Thomas, leads to the degeneracy of art and communication. The play should reflect the cosmic subconscious mind's searching need of and voyage in the sensory world toward complete self-expression. Because of this law, nature evolves toward altruistic ideals, and mankind, toward civilization. Evolutionary regression by individuals and the species can occur, but not without catastrophic consequences.

The playwright should imitate this altruistic standard of nature by dramatizing through the acts of his characters, not private, but racial ideals, such as "ideal heroism, ideal sacrifice, ideal charity, ideal mercy, ideal justice."[14] Dramatizing the "sentiments beneath a race, the sentiments that keep a people's meaning,"[15] he excites the higher instincts of his audience and assists the cosmic mind's evolutionary expression of its altruistic nature. Those plays, however, that stimulate selfish desires in the auditors and reverse these natural laws of psychic evolution, widen the gap between nature and the art work.

Besides imitating nature, drama, as well as all art forms, has as its "primal intention" the communication of emotion.[16] Because emotions are aroused by a bombardment of the instincts, the "basis" or "skeleton" of all plays, even of each act and scene, is conflict, "a triangle, two forces struggling for an object."[17] No motif or event should be presented on the stage just for the interest that will be aroused for it; all material dramatized should induce emotional catalysis in the characters of the play.[18]

The emotions are not just expressed in the play, they are also transmitted to the audience. The dramatized emotion is "understood and sympathized with" by all spectators who possess the instinct from which the emotion was called into existence; a "like, though feebler, emotional state" is reflected in the breasts of the members of the audience.[19] Because of the universality of the instinct of self-preservation, all spectators will react to any emotion stemming from it, but a progressively decreasing number of spectators will be able to understand and thus respond to each higher-level instinct. Thus intellectual topics should be made palatable to the audience by appeal to the basic lower instincts. The "very greatest play is that which reaches from the physical to the spiritual, starting at the lower stratum [*sic*] and extending upward through the various layers of strata to the top."[20]

The idea of the play, firmly present in the public mind, deeply felt by the author, based on the instincts, and dramatized through an arousal of emotion, is the play's "controlling purpose," its theme. Each play requires a theme, which, according to Thomas, is the most important constituent element. Thus a work of art defective in expression still can be considered a great work of art.

Thomas's understanding of the subconscious mind influenced his dramatic technique, as well as his definition of the good and successful play. The imagistic medium of the subconscious and the fact that the eye "deals . . . more directly" with the mind than does the ear[21] led Thomas to emphasize the need for a play to be performed rather than read and to stress its visual elements. He did the latter by focusing on action, which, whenever possible, substituted for dialogue. Themes and motifs in the play were not discussed, but dramatized or led to action. Likewise, techniques, processes, and contrivances possibly unknown to the audience were demonstrated instead of being explained. Lengthy speeches were punctuated with an appeal to the eye; concrete, as opposed to abstract, language was employed. Props were repetitively used, and all the forces and their objectives in the play were expressed in images. Each play had a character exemplifying the theme and a character opposing it. The catalyst for the action of the play was their contention for a physical object or a "person in dispute . . . a character whose life and fortune are to be shaped, heightened or despoiled accordingly as the idea of the play conquers or fails."[22]

The psychically affective nature of imagery and the amenability of the subjective mind to suggestion led Thomas to stress the importance of symbolism, "the strongest thing in human consciousness,"[23] by which most people awaken to the deeper meanings of life. In the theater, meaning is suggested through the symbolic use of character, action, accessories, and settings. Change in the appearance of an actor or his movement is not introduced to provide "variety" but to mark a "change in the actor's condition." The physical surroundings—"every article of furniture, each wall and opening"—are not decorative, but "consonant to the dominant intention of the act or particular division of the play in which the surroundings are established."[24] Lighting should also be used suggestively. Colors can suggest certain moods: yellow prompts gaiety; green, contentment; red, contentment with slight stimulation; brown, fear; violet, sadness; blue, perplexity or mystery; and rose, affection. Moonlight, which combines the blue of mystery and the green of contentment, can be employed to suggest "adoration—where the woman is on the pedestal."[25]

According to Thomas's definition of the drama, it should not only be performed on stage; it should also be performed before an audience. Thomas believed that the successful performance of a play becomes a psychic event, in which an interchange occurs among actors, audiences, and lines. The actors and audience enter into a subjective state, in which the actors at least become favorably disposed to, then identify with, and finally become the roles they play; have confidence in their ability to act; and are relaxed, allowing themselves to become transmitters of the psychic energy outside of themselves. The audience, in turn, accepts the play as real and the suggestions of the play as truthful.

To encourage spectators to believe the play is real, the playwright tries to lull to sleep the audience's conscious mind by using the techniques discussed earlier (dramatizing an idea deeply felt by the audience, imitating nature and its laws, appealing to the instincts and arousing emotions, and fully utilizing the visual medium). He also stills potential objections by the conscious mind by personifying the audience's possibly skeptical attitude to the play's theme and by taking into account the audience's attention span when constructing the scenes and acts of the play. In personifying the skeptical force in the audience, Thomas gave "the public a representative in the cast of characters—a person who should doubt and disbelieve and deny."[26] This character, called by Thomas the "Attorney for the People," is "detached . . . an outsider, a doubter"; he is likable but weak, often called the "familiar 'family friend,' a fine comedy part."[27]

In summary, psychic concepts influenced Thomas's prescriptive definition of the play. The dynamic power of thought influenced his views that the author extrasensorily attracts to himself needed material for his play, that the playwright should dramatize as the theme an idea firmly in the public mind and deeply felt by the author, and that the hub of the play should be conflict. The faculty of instincts inclined Thomas to center the conflict on an attack on instincts and an arousal of emotion; the faculty of mimesis led him to imitate nature and nature's laws and present heroic emotions and ideals in the play. The imagistic language of the subconscious mind prompted him to emphasize the visual medium of the play, to personify all forces in the play, and occasionally to unify the play through focal images. The power of suggestion of the subconscious mind, as well as its imagistic language, affected Thomas's use of character, action, accessories, and setting for suggestive and symbolic purposes. And the psychic nature of a successful performance led him to define the audience as integral to that performance.

Thomas's concept of the subconscious mind also influenced his understanding of the theater's two major services: to instruct by stirring emotions and to serve as a means of vicarious expression. According to Thomas, emotions can die from atrophy, the threat of which was greater in his time than ever before, he thought, because of the monotonous and specialized nature of work in the modern industrial system. Thus Thomas considered drama and the other art forms as extremely valuable for stirring and consequently "keeping the emotions malleable."[28] The most important service of the theater is its vicarious expression of the innumerable, submerged desires in every heart, which are the "survivals from our multifarious inheritance," through their "mimic and inexpensive utterance on the stage by people trained in the art of such expression." These submerged desires include potential for all criminal and heroic tendencies in the human body.[29] Though these tendencies in many cases have been repressed and nearly extinguished by the inhibitions developed with civilization, they "still lie deep in our subconsciousness, like irritating foreign bodies." Children safely express these tendencies through their games—for example, cops and robbers—thus relieving the explosive pressure created by repression; adults can receive the same relief through the vicarious expression of these desires on the stage.

Because of the theater's services and the psychic nature of the play and its performance, the playwright has an imposing moral responsibility. In stirring the audience's emotions, the playwright stimulates the spectators to perform certain types of actions, moral or immoral, heroic or criminal. Consciously or unconsciously, the playwright suggests altruism or selfishness. Willingly or unwillingly, he either assists the cosmic subconscious mind in its evolution or prompts regression from civilization and movement toward animalistic instincts. Unsurprisingly, Thomas called the theater "the strongest factor for suggestion in our modern civilization,"[30] even more potent than the church with its crucifix and incense.

Thomas's playwriting theories and techniques, like his psychic and psychological plays, were founded on firsthand knowledge and serious study. An investigator of psychic and psychological phenomena, Thomas scrutinized the major literature on these subjects, associated with psychic personalities, and was a friend of such leading psychological and psychical researchers as Pierre Janet, James Hyslop (president from 1906 to 1920 of the American Society for Psychical Research), and Hamlin Garland.[31] Thomas explained his theories and methods in his public statements and his autobiography, all written with young playwrights in mind. In eleven prefaces to published plays, he invited the reader into his workshop, explaining each play's construction from inspiration to finished product. The specific influences on other playwrights of Thomas's theories and techniques is untraceable; but his mastery of craft was generally recognized by his peers, as evidenced by the gold medal awarded to him by the American Academy of Arts and Letters. And his pronouncements carried weight: they certainly contributed to a general improvement in American dramatic technique and assisted in drawing the attention of American playwrights to the details of their craft.

Chapter Three

Regional and National Plays

Many of Thomas's original full-length plays are regional studies, often with contemporary national themes. More than local-color sketches, they conceive regions as distinct limbs and organs of the national body and study the evolution of American character through the regional interplay of environment and temperament. Setting often conditions character and action; and physical action generally is subordinated to mental action and to study of character and setting. These plays, without the exaggeration typical of melodrama in Thomas's time and with a sincerity that seemed new to American audiences, did not pioneer the native American play, but they did help establish its place on the American stage. Most representative of Thomas's regional and national plays are *Alabama* (1891), *In Mizzoura* (1893), *Arizona* (1899), *The Copperhead* (1918), and *The Cricket of Palmy Days* (1919).

Formative Influences

Writing in his autobiography of his earliest memories, Thomas primarily recalled northern sympathizers at the outbreak of the Civil War singing "John Brown lies a-moldering in the grave"; his father, a Union captain, riding through the city park amid the chant of "Grant—Grant—Grant"; the "tump-tump-tump-like" heartbeat of a nation and tramp of soldiers to distant Island Number 10 or Vicksburg; and John Wilkes Booth, his father's New Orleans companion during the Civil War, assassinating Abraham Lincoln. Similar historical and political events were part of the Thomas family dinner-table talk, and national news was eagerly awaited and absorbed by the family.

Thomas's in-laws, the Colbys, traced their links to the country's history further back to the days of the Republic. The long-barreled muzzle-loading shotgun hanging over the fireplace of

Thomas's New Rochelle home belonged to Samuel Bainbridge, his wife Lisle's grandmother's grandfather, who had fought in the American Revolution. Commodore William Bainbridge commanded the *Constitution* ("Old Ironsides") to victory over the British frigate *Java.* The Thomas and Colby tradition of service to country continued in Thomas's immediate family. His son, Luke, volunteered for service during World War I. At the age of twenty-three, he was an infantry major in France and commanded a brigade of eight thousand soldiers, while his sister, Glory, drove an ambulance ferrying soldiers from returning ships to hospitals. Thomas, active in politics from 1877 through 1928, sold war bonds.

Thomas was thus well suited to reverberate the country's heartbeat in his plays. He had toured the country many times— as an actor performing in 1883–84 before American audiences in the Midwest, North, and South; as a press agent in 1889 for mind reader Washington Bishop; and afterward as a campaigner stumping in presidential elections. As a reporter he had learned the need of firsthand observation. As a playwright he wrote from his own experience, not from books, often traveling to a place to absorb color and study character and setting. He was always keenly aware of those currents of common interest galvanizing the country.

Alabama (1891)

During the 1880s, antebellum plantation life was frequently glorified in stories in *Century, Harper's,* and other northern magazines. Henry Grady, the *Atlanta Constitution* editor, and others were describing the rise of a progressive New South; and the North in practice was dropping its opposition to white political supremacy in the South. Northerners and southerners alike were beginning to feel that sectional differences, as Jefferson Davis had said in 1888 in his last speech, belonged to the past. In 1891 the country was ready for the theme of *Alabama*—the need for the reconciliation of the North and South after the Civil War.

The theme is symbolized by the love relationships of Captain Davenport and Mrs. Page, and Armstrong and Carey Preston. The relationship of Davenport (apparently a northern railroad president, in actuality Harry, a southerner, son of Colonel Preston) and Mrs. Page had been frustrated during their youth by Colonel Preston; later, when Harry joins the Union forces during the Civil War, father and son become estranged. During the time of the action of the play, Armstrong, a northern agent for Davenport's railroad, plans to elope with his employer's daughter, Carey, whose existence is unknown to Davenport. Davenport prevents the elopement, becomes reunited with Mrs. Page and his father, and blesses the union of his daughter and Armstrong.

A national reconciliation through the use of northern capital to industrialize the South is symbolized by the building of the railroad through the sleepy Alabama bayous. But progress comes slowly to the sluggish Coosa County bayou of the play, where the sun seems to stand still at noon, humanity vegetates, and news is so scarce that the weekly Talladega Sentinel plans to print as its entire front page the diagram of a planned railway route. The effect on frog gigging of damming the bayou is a potential objection to the route.

Northern energy, symbolized by the construction of a railroad, comes to this sleepy bayou. Armstrong, while walking with Carey, switches his cane, cutting off the heads of four-o'clocks. He plans to elope with this engaging but unsophisticated Alabama girl, who has never seen a streetcar, after knowing her for only a week. His employer, Captain Davenport, combines northern industry and a respect for southern traditions. He has built embankments and cities in the wilderness, but sensitive to Colonel Preston's wish to be left alone, he diverts the railway route from this unreconstructed southerner's sleepy bayou.

The union of Armstrong and Carey represents the reunification of the North and South—one rich in industry and capital, the other in natural resources and tradition. And Davenport, president and chief engineer of the Gulf and Midland Railway, represents the economic bridge of cooperation already beginning to join North and South. He explains to Colonel Preston:

The North and South were two sections when they were a forthnight's journey apart by stages and canals. But now we may see the sun rise in Pennsylvania, and can take supper the same day in Talladega.

It is one country. Alabama sends its cotton to Massachusetts—some of it grown very near your graveyards. The garment you have on was woven twenty miles from Boston. Every summer Georgia puts her watermelons on the New York docks. Pennsylvania builds her furnaces at Birmingham. The North took some of your slaves away—yes—but one freight car is worth a hundred of them at transportation. Our resentment, Colonel Preston, is eighteen years behind the sentiment of the day.[1]

Other characters are thematic symbols. Lathrop Page, the *Sentinel* editor, who runs even when the thermometer registers in the nineties, represents the energy of the New South. He is enterprising and has business acumen. Though young, he has secured several town lots and options on property parcels between Talladega and Colonel Preston's plantation, the proposed direction of the railway. Colonel Moberly is the chivalrous southern gentleman of pre–Civil War days slowly adapting to new times. Squire Tucker is the sophisticated, easygoing, good-hearted southerner, seemingly unaffected by the Civil War or the progress of the last fifteen years. Raymond Page, who makes the claim that his cousin Mrs. Page was not legally married so he can obtain her property title, now valuable because of the proposed railroad, is the unscrupulous southerner with none of the virtues of antebellum southern codes of behavior. The villain of the play, he seeks to exploit southerners and northerners alike for his own monetary gain. For his influence on the Missouri Assembly committee on railroads, he requests from Armstrong a kickback of one thousand dollars.

To write a play that would appeal to northerners and southerners, Thomas sketched, not the South shattered by the Civil War, but the romantic South. The plantation's decaying ruin is enchanting. Virginia creepers cover the wall, gateway post, and cannon fragmented during Sherman's march to Atlanta; in the cannon's mouth a meadowlark builds her nest. The southern moon seems brighter and more golden than the northern one. Lush vegetation covers the bayou, and the sweet odor of magnolias permeates the air (and during the performance, even the theater).

Though the Preston plantation, like most of the heavily mortgaged southern plantations, became bankrupt after the Civil

War, Thomas mentions only one of the problems facing the typical plantation owner—the disruption of the labor system when many of the blacks who love Colonel Preston are driven into vagabondage, theft, and ignorance. There is no allusion to the confiscation of all Confederate and many private assets; the institution of unequal confiscatory taxes; the evils of tenant sharecropping and crop-lien arrangements; the lack of diversification of crops; or the soaring public debt in the South, most of it incurred by corrupt carpetbag government. Though the Talladega Light Artillery does not allow a black to get to the caucus and is almost a balance-of-power party in primary elections, it is not an organization of violence such as the Ku Klux Klan was between 1867 and 1869. It does not have even a gun; and Colonel Moberly, its leader, is spoken of affectionately as a bighearted and loyal "old war horse" being pushed by the new generation from his hobbies. "Uncle" Decatur, the faithful Preston black servant who refuses a tip from Armstrong, considers himself a family member.

The play, in its local color, as well as in its theme, characters, and setting, is thoroughly American. Frogs are gigged, and molasses is served at the breakfast table. Southerners are prejudiced against northern men courting southern women. An insult to a woman's honor is cause for a duel. Upon introductions, women's hands are kissed, bows are made, and hats are lifted. Courtesy titles like "mister" and "mistress" are used; and southern hospitality, even to northerners, is quickly offered. The southern dialect is accurate and colorful, particularly Squire Tucker's uneducated slang, uninformed grammar, and local expressions, and Colonel Moberly's complimentary language is often filled with military expressions.

Based on firsthand observation of current American life, *Alabama* also departed from the conventional portraits of hero, heroine, and villain, and the emphasis on physical action of melodrama. Thomas played down the reconciliation of father and son after eighteen years of separation, the first meeting of father and daughter, the union of two lovers against the opposition of a father, and the villainy of Raymond's falsely claiming that Mrs. Page is not a legal wife. Revolting against the playwriting principle of never following a climax with a weaker situation, Thomas draws the curtain to act 1, not when

Raymond Page tells Mrs. Page, "You are not his wife," but after the characters talk the situation over with Squire Tucker. Act 2 does not end with the glass of water flung in Page's face, but with the effect of Page's accusation on Colonel Preston. In act 3, when the elopement is stopped by Davenport and the lover cries, "By what right do you interfere in this affair?" the act does not conclude with Davenport's revelation: "I am her father." Instead, the father reasons gently with the girl and sends her home, escorted by her would-be eloper. Act 4 does not end with the exposure of the villain, who had earlier taken a bribe, or his forced apology; Colonel Preston's slow consent to Armstrong and Carey's marriage; or the reunion of father and son. Armstrong and Carey, Davenport and Mrs. Page, and Colonel Moberly and a new charmer are all happily paired before the curtain falls while Squire Tucker, a mother's boy who had been courting Mrs. Page, murmurs, "Perhaps it wouldn't 'a' been fo' the best . . . with mother leanin' on me." *Alabama*— with its quiet endings, naturalness of incident and realism of character, native quality, and lack of stirring action scenes and declamatory lines—was a progressive step toward a more modern American drama.

In Mizzoura (1893)

The success of *Alabama* led Nathaniel Goodwin, who had appeared almost exclusively in farces, to ask Thomas to write for him a play with a serious starring role. Studying a Goodwin photograph, Thomas decided a gun was necessary to explain the solid confidence animating that slight 150-pound physique and cast Goodwin as a sheriff, Jim Radburn. Drawing upon his St. Louis reportorial friendship with "Jim Cummings," a train robber, and the details of the Cummings robbery, Thomas created Travers, an attractive and suave outlaw whom Radburn would arrest and who would be the sheriff's rival for a girl of finer strain. Following Cummings's trip north to Pike County, Missouri, after the robbery, a journey Thomas had made more than once as a railroad worker, the playwright went to Bowling Green, the setting of the play, for firsthand observation, as did Goodwin after the play was written. Here Thomas listened to a blacksmith talk about Missouri politics, watched him weld a wagon tire, and observed his helper finish a wagon shaft with a draw knife. He put both persons and their activities into the play, as well as other observations.

Though the rough villagers of *In Mizzoura* and the quiet, kindhearted sheriff, Jim Radburn, are romanticized, the depiction of the frontier sheriff is a departure from the usual stage character with his conspicuous bravery and blazing guns. Soft-spoken and reserved, Radburn never draws his two revolvers during the play, but always is calmly and unequivocally in control in dangerous situations. He is also self-sacrificing for the girl he loves. When he learns that Kate Vernon wants to live in Missouri's capital with its broad social opportunity, he withdraws from a political race against her father for nomination to the Missouri legislature. He later sacrifices his horse, a ten-thousand-dollar reward for a train robber's capture, and possibly the respect of the community, even facing possible prosecution, so that the man Kate thinks she loves can escape across the Illinois border.

For characters, Thomas drew, not refined people as in *Alabama,* but common people amid their everyday routines in a state retaining many frontier features. The act 1 curtain rises on the Vernons' impoverished living room. A broken rocker is the most comfortable chair in the house. The window screens, made from mosquito net, are torn from dogs having jumped through them. Foul-smelling dog fennel burns outside the door to smoke off mosquitoes, which are so persistent that Mrs. Vernon, unable to sleep the preceding night, smeared herself with coal oil. Mother and daughter iron, while the sound of the father's hammer rings from the anvil in the adjoining blacksmith shop. On this hot June night, the exhausted Mrs. Vernon cracks the pearl button on her husband's shirt bosom and then fans herself with a frayed palm leaf as she awaits a quart of St. Louis beer, ordered by prescription from the drugstore, because Pike County is dry. Colonel Bollinger sweats through two paper collars.

The play is rich with realistic details. The blacksmith's shop, seen in act 2, includes a forge, bellows, anvil, tub of water, bench with vise, and such tools as a traveler. Assisted by too many idle hands, Jo Vernon heats a steel tire red hot in the forge and then hammers a weld before chilling and fastening the tire on a stagecoach's wagon wheel. His helper, Dave, later shapes a wagon shaft with a draw knife; and concern is raised whether the coke in the shop has impurities, which in the furnace form clinkers, hard fused stony masses. In act 3, Dave and Elizabeth play checkers on a homemade board until news is brought that Travers has shot a Pinkerton detective in the neck. Trying to escape in the drugstore, Travers steps into a perfumery case, stands on a soda counter, and knocks over the store's green lights as he crashes through a window, kicking licorice onto the sidewalk. In act 4, Radburn steels himself in his front yard to meet a mob; behind him spreads rolling country, rich with leafy trees, and a country road winds past a gate.

Like *Alabama, In Mizzoura* is not a play of action, but a play of character. In this most Bret Hartean of Thomas's plays, the characterization is romantic; the villagers are rugged but good-natured and large-hearted. Yet these distinctly American characters are refreshingly untheatrical. The most conventional character, the mustached Travers, in a letter to the St. Louis *Globe Democrat* unconventionally accepts all responsibility for the robbery so that an express-train messenger, Sam Fowler, held as his accomplice, might be released. The unconventional heroine, lolling around the house in fine dress instead of helping to iron clothes or bring milk, has been spoiled by four years of education at a female seminary. She temporarily rejects the sheriff and considers eloping with the polished and well-mannered Travers, whom she does not love as much as she loves his association with the world of broader horizons outside Pike County.

The unconventional hero, Radburn, who carries in his body seven bullets fired by men he has pursued, has never killed a man, though he has shot fifty, winging them in the leg if they were escaping or in the hand if they were drawing a gun. During crises he remains collected. While Colonel Bollinger is reveling in the gossip of Travers's having shot a man and is running in circles searching for his revolver, Radburn quietly asks what the man who shot the Pinkerton detective looks like and where he went. Then telling his sister, Emily, "Come, little gal, we got to go home" and saying to the men, "Better meet at the Court House," he calmly leaves the Vernons'. His nerve and capability of action are suggested, not dramatized. He sits quietly

and confidently in act 4 outside a closet door without a drawn
weapon, waiting for the robber within to storm out. He then
parleys with his rival in low conversational tones and few gestures, as he also does when he without gunplay confronts and
subdues a mob.

Other characters, even the major mob members, are well
differentiated. Dave, the blacksmith's apprentice, who has been
fashioning a set of furniture with his draw knife and will receive
Jo's permission to marry Elizabeth only when he has a "stiddy"
job, is nicely done, as are the Hartean characters Mr. and Mrs.
Vernon. Both are big-boned, somewhat rugged on the exterior,
but generous, quickly adopting the yellow dog found by Radburn, though they already have three dogs too many for their
meager resources. Mrs. Vernon, apprehensive about Kate's relationship with Travers, and Jo, more indulgent in family matters,
are a good contrast, as are Radburn and Travers, and Kate
and her hard-working, slovenly sister, Elizabeth.

The first two acts are primarily character and place studies.
The action in this modified melodrama does not start until act
2, when news is brought that Travers has shot a detective.
Though the play's pace then quickens, Radburn's easy controlled
movement is more prominent than all the bustle of the big
scenes. As in *Alabama,* these scenes are dramatically effective,
particularly Kate's rejecting Radburn, who has anonymously
financed her years at the seminary, because she is better educated
than he; and Radburn's confrontations with Travers and the
mob. The mob, which has come to jail him for loaning his
horse to Travers, ends up cheering him when it learns he helped
Travers for the woman he loves. The curtains for the acts, however, fall during the quietest stage moments, when emotions
rage within the impassive sheriff. Act 2 ends with Radburn,
unsettled and aimless after the rejection, turning in a natural
and undefined sympathy to pet the crippled dog under the helper's bench. Act 3 concludes after Radburn and Travers's confrontation, with Radburn asserting, "You can take my horse, but
I'm d—d if I'll give you my hand." In act 4, when Kate, learning
of Radburn's sacrifice for her, comes to her senses and weeps
on her father's shoulder, the mother urges the sheriff to pursue
her in his hour of victory. "Some other time," he answers,
and the curtain falls.

Like *Alabama, In Mizzoura* minimizes action and highlights character and setting. In Thomas's next major regional play, *Arizona,* setting is still prominent, but the characterization, except for three portraits, is subordinated to the action.

Arizona (1899)

In *Arizona* the handsome, roguish Captain Hodgman, of the Eleventh United States Cavalry, tempts Estrella, married to the older Colonel Bonham and bored by life on the Fort Grant army post, to elope with him. Lieutenant Denton, to whom Colonel Bonham has been like a second father, stops their flight and makes Hodgman surrender the Bonham jewels, the possession of which was Hodgman's primary motive for the elopement. Colonel Bonham, returning unexpectedly to the post, finds Denton along with his wife and the family jewels. To protect Bonham from knowing the truth, Denton confesses to stealing the jewels and resigns from the army.

A few months later, the soldiers, on their way to the border, stop at Henry Canby's ranch. Hodgman is shot by Tony, a vaquero, who has learned of Hodgman's seduction of his love, Lena Kellar; and Denton, now a cowboy, is accused of the killing and arrested. Acquitted at the trial because the fatal bullet is not of the caliber of his gun, Denton is further exonerated by Estrella's confession of her relationship with Hodgman. Denton and Canby's younger daughter, Bonita, plan to marry after he returns from fighting in the Spanish-American War as captain of a contingent of cowboy volunteers. The impression is left that Estrella and Colonel Bonham will reunite.

A summary of the plot fails to account for the popularity of *Arizona,* which ran for 140 consecutive performances in New York and which, Lionel Barrymore estimated, was being performed in 1900 by at least eighty-seven road companies.[2] The plot is melodramatic and conventional, having appeared in Bronson Howard's *Shenandoah* and earlier, but the action is superbly paced to build suspense, and the characters, their dialogue, and the setting are realistic and vivid.

The details of *Arizona* are indebted to Thomas's firsthand observation of ranch and army post life during his 1897 trip to Arizona. From the Bonham's drawing room (act 2)—with

its Mexican loom, simple, old-fashioned furniture, and walls
of deep terra-cotta—to the Canby's dining room (acts 3 and
4)—with its profusion of Apache pottery and woven baskets,
Navajo blankets, and chairs with seats and backs of cowhide—
the settings are realistic. All dwelling walls, including Canby's
courtyard (act 1), are three-foot-thick adobe; window recesses
are deep enough for chairs. The desert, beneath a blistering
sun, is dusty, dry, and harsh; more than a backdrop, it affects
the lives of the characters. The soldiers, repeatedly brushing
alkali dust from their travel-stained uniforms, need stamina in
this demanding environment. Estrella Bonham, recoiling from
the dreariness of the desert, prepares to leave her husband,
the commanding officer of an army post, and escape with Captain
Hodgman to New Orleans.

   Arizona captures the peculiar characteristics of the region.
In the Southwest a man is judged not on his past but on whether
he can sit sixty hours in the saddle, holding a herd that's always
trying to stampede. Anyone who cannot ride a horse may soon
be dead. Women may ride as well as men and are treated with
as much charity as can be rounded up in the Gospel of St.
John. Estrella's foolishness can be forgiven; and Lena, daughter
of a German-born sergeant, can mother an illegitimate child
and later have a respectable marriage.

   Three characters drawn from real life—Canby, a rancher, Bonita, his daughter, and Tony, a vaquero in love with Lena—
break the mold of earlier stage types. Canby's racy talk is filled
with ranching expressions and analogies, as well as the wisdom
of experience. A foil to Bonham's narrow definition of himself
as a soldier, he is as expansive as his ranch—from end to end
a two-day ride in the saddle. Unlike his peppery wife, he is
justifiably lax in supervision of the spirited Bonita and judges
a man according to his character rather than his clothes. A successful rancher rarely beaten in the race to deliver cattle first
to the government or the Indians, Canby can make $100,000
one year and go broke the next, depending on the amount of
rain and the tariff on Mexican cattle. He is hospitable and generous, making Lieutenant Denton, who has informed him of his
intentions to marry Bonita, half-partner in his ranch.

   Bonita, breezy and invigoratingly independent, can talk man-
to-man to the colonel. A skilled horsewoman, she has had her

rough edges polished at a San Francisco school. Tony frequently plays the mandolin, wooing Lena. Naively indifferent to English profanity, having learned the good and bad together, he can conclude his lover's declaration with "and damn to hell my soul, I love you!"

Bonham, not peculiarly a southwestern figure, is much more than the jealous husband of a much younger wife. As a man of action, frequently rushing to attend to his duties, he is not in touch with Estrella's emotional needs. He never takes her to dances or the towns and can't understand her reasons for crying. An old war campaigner rusting from inactivity until the *Maine* was sunk in the Havana harbor, he is too strict in his observation of regulations and discipline. Riding with his troops to catch a train for service in the Spanish-American War, he makes only a water and cinch-tightening stop at Canby's ranch. He refuses Canby's offer of champagne for all his officers and instead has coffee sent to them. After Hodgman is shot, he reduces Sergeant Kellar, Lena's father, in rank, pending an inquiry. He orders the pursuit of Tony, who escapes on horseback after confessing to the shooting, though nearly all on stage applaud his freedom and an Arizona jury would acquit him of murder. And he refuses to forgive Estrella until he returns from the war, although she now knows she loves Bonham and is contrite for her foolishness. His dramatic effectiveness stems as much from internal conflict as from his pivotal role in the action. Particularly jealous of Denton, he is torn in act 2 between believing either that his wife is unfaithful or that Denton, like a son to him, is a thief and, in act 4, between loving his wife and not wanting to say anything he may later want unsaid.

The characterizations of Denton and Hodgman are not full-bodied. Denton is the loyal, honorable officer, sacrificing his reputation to save Bonham from learning of his wife's indiscretions. He is patriotic, leaving the girl he loves because his West Point messmates and the flag, to which he was taught always to take off his hat, are going to Cuba. The black-mustached Hodgman, nearly expelled from the Corps Cadets and involved in a Leavenworth scandal, is a complete villain. The father of an illegitimate child whom he refuses to support or acknowledge as his own, he toys with women's affections for his own amusement. He tries to seduce the sister of the woman he plans to lure away from her husband. Constantly, even while dying, he casts suspicion on Denton. His villainy is logically motivated: he feels discriminated against by what he considers to be army favoritism, political promotions, and the epaulette that stands between him and marriage to Estrella. Though Denton and Hodgman and others in the play are stock characters, they are dramatically effective, for characterization and other elements are subordinated to the plot, which, though conventional, is animated by fast-paced, tense, and suspenseful action. Near the end of act 1, Hodgman turns sharply on Denton, who has espied the former kissing Estrella's hand. In act 2, Hodgman, who has procured Estrella's diamonds for their escape to New Orleans, is halted in the Bonham's drawing room doorway by Denton, who pulls his revolver and takes the jewels. Urging Estrella never to see Hodgman again, Denton is interrupted by the arrival of Bonham and is discovered hiding behind a curtain with the jewels on his person. In act 3, when Denton tells Canby that Bonita has accepted his marriage proposal, the rancher's hand darts into his pistol pocket. Denton's hand as quickly reaches for his revolver as Canby draws out his tobacco pouch. Later in the act Denton strikes Hodgman across the face with a sombrero, at the same time drawing his revolver. Tony, who has learned that Hodgman has seduced his sweetheart, Lena, fires from the pantry door, and Denton accidentally discharges his gun into the floor. Hodgman falls, claiming Denton has shot him; and Bonham orders Denton arrested.

Whereas the first three acts, particularly 2 and 3, are filled with physical action, act 4 is dominated by mental action—concern about Denton's and Estrella's fate. Tension is heightened by the urgency of the cavalry's journeying to Cuba. Bonham has twenty minutes to turn Denton or some guilty party with the facts over to the civil authorities. The cowboy volunteers for the Spanish-American War, for whom Denton was to serve as captain, are restless. Canby is balking at the martial law Bonham has placed on his ranch while Bonham hurriedly examines Kellar and Denton, and the doctor operates to remove the ball lodged in the dying Hodgman's shoulder. Suspicion is deflected from Denton to the innocent Lena until Tony, confessing to the shooting, jumps on Bonita's horse and escapes. As Estrella beseeches her husband to forgive her, Bonham hears the bugle call to leave and must ride to war. Though *Arizona* has a hero and villain and dramatic confrontations, the play is refined melodrama. Act 1 does not end with a clash between Hodgman and Denton, though Denton replies to Hodgman in a defiant undertone, for Estrella intervenes and escorts Hodgman to the supper table. The curtain in act 2 falls upon the silent picture of the young officer writing his resignation at the direction of the man whose honor he has saved at the expense of his own. Act 3 ends not with the shooting of Hodgman but with Denton being arrested amid a chorus of exclamations and questions from the cowboys. And act 4 does not end with the union of Colonel Bonham and Estrella, but with Bonham's picking up the rose that had been fastened at Estrella's throat, symbolizing the probability of their eventual reconciliation.

The dialogue is superior to that in *Alabama* and *In Mizzoura*. Without soliloquies and asides, it is terse, at times racy, often quick-witted, and always effective. Contrasts in the play—Denton's diffident, Hodgman's aggressive, and Tony's romantic wooing; the freedom of the ranch and the restrictions of the army post; Canby's bigness of character and Bonham's narrow definition of himself by his duties as a colonel—are well contrived. *Arizona,* the Thomas play most liked by all kinds of playgoers, is his best work before 1900.

The Copperhead (1918)

No manager would produce the original version of *The Copperhead,* Thomas's three-act play based on Frederick Landis's novel *The Glory of His Country.* At the suggestion of his son, Thomas revised the story in which Milt Shanks, who had been hated by his long-dead family and has been ostracized by his Illinois neighbors for his supposed southern sympathies during the Civil War, foils unscrupulous plots against the congressional campaign of his granddaughter's suitor. Excising the political melodrama, Thomas added both a contest between the granddaughter and a girl of lesser ability but of respectable ancestry for a local schoolteaching position and the concern of a congressman's mother that her son find a suitable wife. Dividing the play into epochs, one during the Civil War and the other during the time of Landis's book, Thomas included local color from his memories of primitive Illinois scenes and the simple, direct speech and dialect of its people, as well as from his vivid recollections of the Civil War. He captured the stir of the country preparing for and embarking on war: the bitterness among neighbors in pro-Union Illinois and the border states of Kentucky and Missouri; the women cutting and sewing uniforms; the young boys molding *Minenwerfer* balls and making cartridges for muzzle-loading rifles; the babies and household duties to be looked after while the men were gone; fairs to raise money for hospital equipment; the unreliable news from the front; and the women's uninformed but sharp criticism of the conduct of the war.

Much of the effectiveness of the first two acts, occurring in 1861 and 1863, stems from this local color and characterization. Grandma Perley and Ma Shanks, modeled on Thomas's militant grandmother and his sacrificing, patient mother, are studies in contrast; the sharp-tongued Grandma Perley, who had molded bullets for Andrew Jackson's troops during the War of 1812, dominates the scenes with her broad physical movements and decisive opinions, whereas Ma Shanks responds to the seeming apostasy of her husband with few words, restrained emotion, but occasional scorn. Her husband has to endure silently her reproaches, as well as those of their neighbors, and the shame of his sixteen-year-old son, Joey, who, against the wishes of his mother, eagerly goes to war. His dramatically effective tension is revealed by his awkwardness in professing southern sympathies, his uneasy joining in the spying activities of the Knights of the Golden Circle, and his struggle amid the reproaches of family and friends not to blurt out the truth of his service as a northern spy. Having been freed in act 2 from a prison sentence for murder, he returns home on the evening of the day on which the news of Grant's capture of Vicksburg reaches his hometown. As a far-off church bell rings in celebration, a soldier brings him news of his son's death and the boy's dying wish that his father not be allowed to see him. The rift between Milt and his wife widens.

The second epoch of the play presented an actor's opportunity, for Shanks and three of his associates are forty years older than in 1861 and the actress who played Ma Shanks reappears as her own granddaughter. Grandma Perley, Ma Shanks, and Joey—among the four most interesting characters in the first section—are dead, so new interest had to be developed in the middle of the play and the two sections had to be associated through surviving characters and their memories. Thomas accomplishes both objectives by creating the characters of the granddaughter and her suitor and having Shanks's apparent southern sympathies injure her chances of becoming a schoolteacher. Milt's love for his only surviving relative breaks down his long silence, maintained at first because of the possibility of revenge by those who may have felt betrayed by Shanks and later by the habit of silence.

To conjure the spirit of Lincoln when Shanks tells of the midnight interview with the president, during which Lincoln asked for a sacrifice greater than death, Thomas appeals to the eye, as well as to the ear. Shanks takes from a mantel a plaster life mask of Lincoln and places it under a lamp next to a plaster cast of Lincoln's hand. "A bigger man," says Milt, drawing attention to the cast of the large hand that had signed the Emancipation Proclamation, "bigger'n me in every way." Out of a box Shanks takes a yellowing letter written from Lincoln to him thanking him for his patriotism during the Civil War; he also produces a handkerchief flag, similar to the one he placed his hand on when Lincoln swore him into the Secret Service.

The spectator has been prepared for the use of the mask and hand cast by earlier allusions and references to Lincoln. Shanks's monologue is interrupted by pauses and occasional responses from listeners. The effect in this last scene of the play—one of the "most moving utterances of our stage," according to Arthur H. Quinn[3]—is as if Lincoln had entered the room.

The Cricket of Palmy Days (1919)

The mellow three-act *The Cricket of Palmy Days,* a drama of period and characterization, re-creates California mining-camp life during the gold rush and the beginnings of a native American drama. In Ma Curley's Lone Tree Bar, a theatrical troupe's ingenue, Cricket, jigs on an improvised stage with candles for footlights, while red-shirted miners toss gold dust and hard money at her dancing feet. As Big Lil, One-Eyed Conover, Leavenworth, and other characters with as colorful names watch, the troupe's blackened-face Banjo King, Robinson, delivers minstrel and vaudeville patter and sings George Christy's "Uncle Ned."

Kaintuck, whose characterization was inspired by Wilton Lackaye's makeup of a full-bearded miner in a western bar for a 1918 Lambs Club sketch, is the mining camp pet. This mellow and affable but authoritative miner, who had been actor Edwin Forrest's valet sometime between 1831 and 1848, frequently quotes Shakespeare in everyday conversation and fancies himself in Forrest's roles. He is cynical toward all actresses, having separated from his wife, a strolling actress, whom he suspects of providing him with an illegitimate child fathered by Forrest. He seeks to prevent the love match of his partner, David Woodford Crockett, and Cricket until he discovers that she, strikingly resembling a miniature ivory portrait of his mother, is his legitimate daughter.

Thomas breathes life into the performance of this traveling theatrical troupe at Lone Tree and into the rough bewhiskered miners, who are starved for outside entertainment and the sight of a beautiful girl. Their talk is spiced with mining and draw-poker expressions, as in the climax of act 2, when Bud Farrell threateningly bids Kaintuck "good evening" and Kaintuck replies, "I sees your 'good evening' and I raises you 'au revoir.'" Kaintuck and the other miners have hair-trigger emotions and dispense with judges and lawyers in favor of personal or vigilante settlement of differences. *The Cricket of Palmy Days,* however, like Ma Curley's barroom, where only one man is shot for every ten at the bars at Arroya, Alta Vista, and Red Gulch, is nearly a scandal for its respectability. Guns are drawn only infrequently and never fired on stage; the most melodramatic scene, an attempted kidnapping, is played off stage; and after act 2 the two villains—a faro dealer, with high boots and a taste for all the women, and a miner enamored of the juvenile lead of the troupe—disappear as a threat to the hero, never incurring retribution.

Thomas's story of the 1850s re-creates the youth of native American drama. With an adoring audience of miners but with-

out a stage, Kaintuck is a mining-camp Edwin Forrest, the first
native-born American actor to gain enduring fame. Cricket is
modeled on the first native-born American actress to win international acclaim, Lotta Crabtree, whose performances Thomas had
seen during his youth in her annual St. Louis engagements.
And the Banjo King's entertainment was based on Thomas's
memory and study of minstrels, who played banjos, fiddles, tam-
bourines, and bones, and offered comedy routines, variety acts,
sentimental songs, and dancing.

Kaintuck's reciting of a line from *The Gladiator,* and the names
of his mining claim, the "Metamora," and his partner, David
Woodford Crockett (the first and last names being the title of
Frank H. Murdoch's 1872 American frontier play)—all mirror
the rise of public interest in plays about America written by
Americans. Kaintuck's frequent quotations from *Hamlet, Anthony
and Cleopatra,* and *As You Like It,* and the stage mother's reciting
from an adaptation of *The Old Curiosity Shop* reflect the perennial
popularity of Shakespeare and Charles Dickens during the palmy
days of the American theater. Kaintuck's reverence for the playhouse, despite his barbed allusions to the acting profession and
the intimate reception given the barnstorming performers, suggests a time when America took its drama seriously—when stock
actors, even playgoers and readers, occasionally quoted lines
dignified in diction and thought from Shakespeare and other
playwrights, and when playgoers regarded their favorite actors
as leaders and the theater as an educational institution, dissemi-
nating information and opinion.[4]

Minor Regional Plays

Several of Thomas's regional plays—*The Hoosier Doctor*
(1898), *Colonel George of Mount Vernon* (1898), *Colorado* (1901),
and *Rio Grande* (1916)—did not receive critical and public acclaim. *The Hoosier Doctor,* depicting small-town life in Indiana,
is Thomas's most biographical play. It includes caricatures of
his father as Julius Willow, the jack-of-all-trades who becomes
a doctor late in life, and his grandmother as the termagant
mother-in-law, critical of Doctor Willow's administering to pa-
tients too poor to pay for his service. The efforts of Willow's
three grown daughters, who help support the family and put

Julius through medical school, parallel Thomas's own family contributions.

Willow, a timorous but loving father and a caring physician, has just graduated with honors from medical school after failing in nearly every other business. He avoids the grocer, whom he owes $11.40, and hides from his mother-in-law the news of his marriage to a widow in the town. His clandestine attempt to visit the widow at night under pretense of sitting up with a sick patient leads to scandal. Except for the stage convention of the adopted child who inherits a fortune, Thomas's play stages what audiences and reviewers considered to be real-life people talking naturally and a truthful picture of American life in the Midwest.

Colonel George of Mount Vernon, set in 1757, liberally adapts history and biography. Colonel Innes's neglected wife, Sally, is presented as the biographical "lowland beauty" to whom Washington as an adolescent wrote verses in unrequited love. Virginia's Governor Robert Dinwiddie, historically Washington's political foe and supporter of Colonel Innes for commander-in-chief of Virginia's militia, through dramatic license accuses Washington falsely of treason and plotting to assassinate the governor.

The play displays Washington's virtues, though Sally, imagining herself in love with him, places him in situations that appear to compromise his intended marriage to Martha Custis. He seems congenitally honest, even when common sense would dictate that Martha should not have straight answers to her questions about his association with Sally. He is graciously hospitable, even to Dinwiddie, who has initiated a warrant for his arrest. He lacks ambition, never promoting his appointment as commander-in-chief and willing to serve under any honorable man. He is a natural and respected leader of men: when news arrives of an attack on the frontier, the soldiers refuse to fight under any other leader, causing the Assembly to elect Washington as commander-in-chief and Dinwiddie to withdraw his charge of treason.

Colorado, based on Thomas's trip to Colorado mines, fails to focus because of too many plot threads and attention to five love relationships. Years before the action of the play, Austin had escaped to Colorado to avoid a five-year sentence for hitting his colonel, Kincaid, who had sexually grabbed his sister. Tom Doyle had also come to Colorado when doctors advised its climate for his wife's health; he had bought from Staples, a gambler, fifty thousand acres of desert advertised as a ranch. The plot of this melodrama, in which Kincaid and Staples force Austin to sell a two-thirds share in his promising mine, is contrived and implausible. When the Austin mine floods and overflows, irrigating nearby property, Doyle becomes a millionaire. After buying the Denver National Bank, he proves from transaction records that Staples and Kincaid had used Austin's money to buy a majority share in a prospering neighboring mine. Freezing their bank assets, he starts legal action for the restitution of Austin's money. By means of a bullet hole made by his daughter, Kitty, through an envelope addressed to Kincaid, Doyle also proves Kincaid knew Austin had been pardoned before he blackmailed him with the threat of exposure.

Rio Grande, for which Thomas absorbed local color firsthand, is similar in plot to *Arizona.* The play has conventional melodramatic trappings: a woman, who has married an older man to please a dying parent, is blackmailed into submitting to an orderly who spied on her love tryst with a young lieutenant; she tries to drown herself in the Rio Grande; the lieutenant places a pistol to his temple and pulls the trigger; and the husband, the military post commander, learning the truth, kills the orderly. In Nan, the repentant wife who realizes she loves her husband, Thomas has created a woman's portrait equal to those of his men.

A Mirror to America

What was American character, manners, dress, and speech like in a certain locale in a certain year? Thomas tried to answer that question in all of his plays, whenever possible, by traveling to the locale. In primitive Bowling Green, Missouri, Thomas discovered *In Mizzoura*'s paper collars, linen duster, dog fennel, and even the window that Travers would break through after shooting a Pinkerton detective. Henry C. Canby, the rancher in *Arizona,* is more a robust frontiersman than was his original, Henry C. Hooker, but hundreds of his picturesque, simple, and direct lines are Hooker's own words. Canby's courtyard and dining room are so realistically re-created on stage that Hooker was identified by some as the model of Thomas's rancher. The Talladega townspeople of *Alabama* talked accurately in the southern dialect of 1880. The Bowling Green inhabitants pronounced the state's name "Mizzoura," as it appeared on territorial charts.

In most cases, Thomas's plays were topical, often on a national scale. The theme in *Alabama* of the reconciliation of North and South was ready for public acceptance in the theater not during the 1880 of the play's setting but in 1891, when the play was produced nationwide to overflowing crowds. *Arizona,* with its cavalry and cowboy volunteers riding toward the Spanish-American War, was produced in Chicago in 1899 during that war. The regional play *Rio Grande* was produced in 1916, when Thomas's son, Luke, was a cavalry lieutenant on the Texas border guarding against the raids of Mexican guerrilla Pancho Villa. In the 1918 production of *The Copperhead,* the ill feeling in 1861 between northern sympathizers and Copperheads, reluctant to go to war when the North had not been invaded, seemed like reportorial accounts of the parallel conditions in America in 1917.

Thomas's plays are thoroughly American, not primarily because they photograph setting, character, and period, but because they study the interaction of temperament and environment, and the resulting regional evolution of American character. In *Alabama,* sweltering summers make the motion of the South unhurried and its characters sluggish or stately. In *Arizona,* the desolate desert shapes character and motivates action. In the Far West where women were scarce, a woman's social standing, no matter how wrong her past, was established as soon as she married. In *Arizona,* Lena and Estrella can be forgiven for their sexual misdirections. In *In Mizzoura,* Mrs. Vernon is her husband's coworker and pal. In *Alabama,* Carey and Mrs. Page are regarded with chivalrous attention.

Because his plays studied the interaction of environment and temperament, Thomas's plots are usually background glue for character and period studies. Action is subdued, situations and traditional climaxes are scarce, and curtains usually fall during quiet moments when a character's emotions rage within. This refining of melodrama and the serious study of the relationship between character and environment make Thomas's plays different from frontier plays, such as Frank Murdoch's *Davy Crockett* (1877) and Bartley Campbell's *My Partner* (1879), and Civil War plays, such as Bronson Howard's *Shenandoah* (1888), William Gillette's *Held by the Enemy* (1886) and *Secret Service* (Philadelphia, 1895), and David Belasco's *The Heart of Maryland* (1895).

The Cricket of Palmy Days, scandalously respectable for a frontier play, calls attention to Thomas's refinement of melodrama, as well as his bridging of the gap between early native American drama and post–World War I modern drama. This last in Thomas's series of distinctly American plays was performed one year before the production of Eugene O'Neill's *The Emperor Jones. Alabama,* the first play in the series, was produced in 1891, when foreign plays, their adaptations, and imitations— as well as men with electric noses and explosive cigars, and other farce-comedy characters—dominated the American stage. With its seemingly real people and talk, and its current and electric theme, *Alabama* was like a breath of fresh air. Thomas never did write the great American play, but he never stopped writing American plays. In the frequency and breadth of his treatment of American themes, characters, and settings, he is the most "American" playwright before Eugene O'Neill.

Chapter Four

Political and Socioeconomic Plays

Before the rise of muckraking literature (usually dated from the January 1903 issue of *McClure's Magazine*), few cries for political and socioeconomic reform had been sounded in American drama, fiction, or poetry. Though dramatists Charles Klein in *The Lion and the Mouse* (1905) and Edward Sheldon in *The Boss* (1911)—as well as popular magazines, "yellow-journal" newspapers, and novelists—contributed to the literature of exposure after January 1903, none of the early-twentieth-century protest plays contains a profound study of American politics and economics or is based on firsthand knowledge. Thomas's *New Blood* (1894), which advocates the stewardship of money and the marriage of capital and labor, and *The Capitol* (1895), which studies the illegal and unconstitutional deflections of the nation's legislative system, are the only American plays before the 1930s to advocate a rethinking of the country's socioeconomic and political foundations.[1] They are thematic plays, preceding the rise of American problem drama by at least eleven years. They take a stand on contemporary issues, such as the right of labor to strike, tariffs, and the illegality and abuses of trusts. As America's first serious socioeconomic and political plays, they are neglected landmarks in American drama history.

Thomas's Political Development and Involvement

Thomas's political and socioeconomic dramas, like his regional and national ones, are rooted in his early environment: in the family that thought nationally and respected democratic leaders and good citizenship, and in his experience as a page in the

Missouri and Washington legislatures, as a railroad clerk for seven years, and at nineteen as the youngest master workman in the history of the Knights of Labor. For forty-two years— from 1877, when he was a Labor Reform party candidate for circuit court clerk, through 1928, when he supported the Democratic party's presidential nominee—Thomas was active in the political arena. During these years he spoke in every presidential campaign and occasionally in state elections, and was active in local politics. He played a major role in the campaigns of William Jennings Bryan and Woodrow Wilson. In 1908 at the Democratic National Convention, he seconded Bryan's nomination and became a nationally recognized political figure. For his contributions to Woodrow Wilson's 1912 campaign, he was offered the ambassadorship to Belgium, which he declined, as he did all other offers of political office that would interfere with playwriting.

Thomas's political and socioeconomic stances primarily responded to post–Civil War abuses created when the replacement of hand labor with machine production in manufacturing and the growth of a nationwide network of railroads and available capital led to the industrialization of America. This industrialization within one generation and the absence of income tax and inheritance tax laws created huge fortunes for Andrew Carnegie, John D. Rockefeller, and other captains of industry. For others, it brought hard times. In 1896, one-eighth of the country's people controlled seven-eighths of its wealth. In every political campaign in which he spoke, Thomas supported the income tax. He advocated the right of workers to strike and called for the federal regulation of the trusts and for an end to laissez-faire economics. His political and socioeconomic remedies, expressed on the stage as well as the political platform, seemed radical in the early 1890s and liberal during the Progressive Era (1901 till 1917), when many of his ideas were supported by liberal Republicans and Democrats. By the 1920s, however, he seemed in some ways politically conservative, probably because of his age, financial status, and participation in the campaign for the repeal of the Eighteenth Amendment. Whereas in 1910 he had asserted the need of government intervention in the marketplace, maintaining that the 52 percent rise in living costs from 1897 to 1910 was due to the combining of manufac-

turers to preserve high prices and high tariffs,[2] in a 1924 letter
to Franklin Delano Roosevelt he urged a "return to the utmost
emphasis on local self-government."[3] Only in foreign affairs,
he wrote in 1922, should government be centralized.
Throughout his life, Thomas believed in constitutionalism
and the sanctity of the Bill of Rights. Like Thomas Jefferson,
the seminal influence on Thomas's political philosophies,
Thomas opposed censorship, insisted upon the separation of
church and state, and promoted a philanthropic view of man
and society. He consistently championed equal opportunity, a
more equitable distribution of the country's wealth, and a society
without class distinctions.

Thomas's Major Plays

Thomas's political conscience impelled him to help shape the
Democratic party platforms and to campaign for them. It also
found expression in his plays, many of which continued the
American stage tradition before 1900 of dramatizing politics
and socioeconomics comically, farcically, and melodramatically.
Winfield Farragut Gurney, in *For Money* (1892), farcically stages
a counterfeit strike of his own railroad only to incite mob rule,
which he, as a colonel, is ordered to suppress. In *Colonel Carter
of Cartersville* (1892), a southern gentleman comically practices
pre–Civil War chivalry in the hardheaded worlds of finance
and business in the 1890s. The unproduced *Pittsburgh* is a melodrama of spectacle. Rioters rush a jail in act 4, turn a cannon
on a train engine, and light a barrel of oil to roll onto a railway
roundhouse. Police assisted by the Philadelphia militia fight the
mob.

Before 1900, politics and socioeconomics also served as an
element of plot or characterization and occasionally as incidental
criticism. In Thomas's *In Mizzoura,* for example, Sheriff Radburn's withdrawal from a legislative race because he is in love
with his political opponent's daughter furthers plot and makes
more believable his later aiding in the escape of a train robber,
whom Kate fancies she loves. In *Arizona,* the unpredictable
beef tariff, sometimes so high a Mexican heifer cannot climb
over it, is criticized, as is Congress for its role in setting up
tariffs.

Thomas's *New Blood* and *The Capitol,* however, break with stage tradition. These first thematic studies of economics and politics in American drama stage and take a stand on burning issues of the day: capital-labor relations, trust formations, protective tariffs, and the influence of moneyed interests and the Catholic church on national legislation. Their characters and events stand for aspects of contemporary problems and suggest solutions to those problems. Even the love relations usually develop the play's theme.

New Blood (1894). *New Blood* is not a class play—though signs of potential capital-labor conflict are evident in act 2—but a drama of the conflict between the irresponsible and the humane use of money. Cortland Crandall, the founder of Crandall Company, seeks to form a trust of farm machinery and implement manufacturers to raise prices, reduce production, and lay off workers. His son, Van Buren, familiar with labor conditions, having worked himself up from factory hand to general manager of Crandall Company, opposes his father at the meeting of these manufacturers and votes against this illegal "association of interests." Later he has constructed for the company's one thousand employees a model village with a school, library, and theater.

Cortland Crandall represents the traditional capitalist, indifferent to the welfare of his employees. Van Buren represents the capitalist who is a custodian of his money. Others in the play stand for the frivolous use of capital. Reverend Ferguson Clarke, a fashionable minister, requests money from Cortland for the building of a parsonage clubhouse, including a sideboard and possibly a pool table. The social-climbing Mrs. Crandall schemes to have Theodore, her foppish son from an earlier marriage to a Virginian for whom she had been a housekeeper, inherit Crandall's money. Her life-style suggests how that money would be wasted. Wearing an elegant house dress in act 1, she shows off her slippers from Cairo, like the ones worn by the wives of desert sheiks. Her evening gown in act 3 is as exquisite as her laced carriage gown in act 1 with its puffed sleeves, collar of turquoise ornaments, and skirt front of huge velvet bows, accompanied by a white-laced flared-brim hat, trimmed with turquoise velvet bows. Her Skye terrier, Flossy, is first bleached by hairdressers and then dyed black.

Like Mrs. Crandall and Reverend Clarke, Barstow Adams, a Chicago millionaire and Van Buren's friend, is nonproductive at the beginning of the play. His money, inherited from his father's investment in palace train cars, allows him to be a man of the world—to travel and buy exotic gifts for his friends: slippers from Cairo for Mrs. Crandall and kimonos from Japan for Van Buren and Gertrude. Before his conversion, signaled by his investment of several million dollars to relocate the Crandall factory closer to its markets and to build a village for the factory employees, Barstow is negatively good. His wealth does not lower the living conditions of the workers, but it does not improve them either.

The evil of Mrs. Crandall and Clarke is the play's most unpardonable. They are unproductive parasites who exploit the productive only so they can mirror themselves more fashionably in the eyes of the New York four hundred. Mrs. Crandall married Cortland for his money and flirts with the minister while her husband is dying. The minister, who would use Cortland's money to recruit converts by making the church a club, disguises his interest in Mrs. Crandall by courting Cortland's daughter, Gertrude.

Cortland also acts from self-interest. He has more money than he needs, but his greed prompts him to spearhead the formation of a trust, which would throw out of work probably three-quarters of the nation's farm equipment laborers. His myopia in business affairs carries over to his family relations. Jealous of his much younger wife, he commands his daughter, Gertrude, who loves Adams, to become engaged to Reverend Clarke. The command is authoritative, because it is Cortland's deathbed wish. He also plans to disinherit Van Buren, who genuinely loves him, for his son's opposition to the merger.

Cortland's sins are pardonable, however. He loves his daughter; he was proud of his son before their confrontation, granting him 25 percent of the company's capital stock. He has contributed to the country's productivity. He can be saved, because his wrongheaded actions are fed by a philosophy of self-interest, which can be altered. The deathbed counseling of his hometown pastor, Joshua Sawyer, the admirable foil to the minister who is not a shepherd, cleanses his soul and perceptions, allowing him to see Van Buren's economic stand as just. His death from an incurable disease in act 3 represents the inevitable death of the incurable view that money provides freedom without responsibility. As the father of Van Buren, he is a necessary link in the historical evolution of altruistic capitalism. *New Blood* was America's first serious socioeconomic play. Economic subject matter in earlier American plays had been in the background, as is the strike in Bronson Howard's *Baron Rudolph* (1887), or had served as the impetus for personality clashes, as in Howard's *The Henrietta* (1887). Economics had been treated melodramatically, comically, even satirically, but not sympathetically and seriously.

In *New Blood,* however, Thomas Kerwin, a Crandall Company master mechanic and union representative, having participated in twenty strikes, knows of their necessity: court relief against combinations is usually ineffective, for the company's books are reported as "lost." He also knows the costliness of a strike, near the end of which a family may be sustained for a week with no more than the table scraps from Van Buren's breakfast with Barstow Adams in act 2. At the meeting of the manufacturing representatives, he does not dispute the right of employers to band together to keep wages low; workers can compensate by unionizing. But a pool—such as those in the sugar-refining, coal, and whiskey industries—leads to massive layoffs, so he threatens a strike if there is a consolidation.

New Blood displays the safeguards and strategies of capital-labor and capital-capital confrontations. The union is not represented by a single leader but by a committee, to protect against the bribing of a union official. To avoid legal interference, the would-be trust plans to lease and sublease its factories to the Crandall Company. Van Buren, who approves of the union but does not belong to it, is able to outvote his father in the board of directors meeting, because he has been entrusted with proxies of 30 percent of the company's stock outside the family to meet unexpected crises. The other farm equipment manufacturers try to bankrupt the Crandall Company by reducing their price list by 50 percent on every item sold by the company. Aided by Adams's investment, Van Buren moves the company from Rochester, New York, to Illinois on the bank of the Mississippi River to gain a marketing advantage over his competitors in New York, Ohio, and Michigan. The Mississippi River serves as a highway to the Gulf and the South American market, and the markets in the Dakotas and the Midwestern grain belt are only a short haul. *New Blood* not only studies the country's socioeconomic problems, it offers a solution to those problems. The Crandall's Fifth Avenue New York home, a house divided, stands for the division of the nation on the trust issue during the early 1890s. In forming combinations, capitalists, says *New Blood*, have disinherited their hard-working sons—the laborers—whose industry is responsible for the production of capital. More ambitious than *Alabama*, which assisted in the reconciliation of the North and South after the Civil War, *New Blood* seeks an end to the bloodshed between capital and labor by perceiving the two as family members. Labor should not seek to limit capitalists' profits: Kerwin thinks unions should not interfere with companies banding together to fix prices, tariffs, and markets. On the other hand, the capitalists need to share some of their profits by caring for the basic needs of the laborers, as in the construction of the model village of Crandall, Illinois. The resulting good will between capital and labor is expressed in act 4 by the Crandall employees' gift to Van Buren of a golden key to their village, mostly made from bits of gold contributed by the workers, including at least a dozen wedding rings from women who had nothing else to give. The marriage of Van Buren and minister Sawyer's daughter in the same act and the prospective marriages of Barstow and Gertrude, and Dr. Clarke and Mrs. Crandall, call forth the good spirits attending this new relationship.

New Blood should have been a landmark in American theatrical history. It was not. Audiences, so polarized in the early 1890s by the burning trust issue and frequent reports of capital-labor confrontations, misinterpreted the play's central conflict to be that of capital and labor instead of humane and selfish capitalism. Labor sympathizers, overall, applauded act 2 in which Van Buren opposes the merger, but found act 3, which presented the Crandall family's domestic matters, anticlimactic. They would have preferred to see act 2 after seeing act 3 and felt the play should have more melodrama. Middle- and upper-class patrons generally tended to feel that the pastors' rivalry in administering to Cortland and his death on stage were tasteless and thought the socioeconomic theme impaired a delightful drawing room comedy.

In Chicago, where the suppression of the Pullman strike had abetted labor sympathy, the play was so successful that manager A. M. Palmer opened the 1894 season at his Broadway theater with *New Blood* and announced his intention to produce that season American plays only, including Thomas's *The Capitol.* In New York, where the theater patron was likely to be more sympathetic toward capital than to labor, the play failed. Patrons were insulted by the unflattering portraits of Mrs. Crandall and Reverend Clarke, certainly the weakest characterizations in the play. Mrs. Crandall is too much a wicked painted woman, Reverend Clarke, too much a fashionable minister. Thomas, who had to quit school to help support his family, knew New York's upper class from a distance. Mrs. Crandall and Reverend Clarke are stock characters; they lack the humanity of the play's other characters. The masculine Barstow, however, was drawn from firsthand observation, as was the brother-sister relationship of Van Buren and Gertrude. Barstow's wooing of Gertrude contains some of Thomas's best dialogue between the sexes. The other dialogue is crisp and witty and effortlessly reveals character and furthers plot. The plot is well constructed, except for act 4, which primarily serves to tie up loose ends and provide the conventional happy ending.

New Blood, about the need of stewardship of money, was a daring play, grappling with economic ills of the time. Four years before its production, amid estimates that 1 percent of the country's people possessed more wealth than the other 99 percent combined, humanitarian Jacob Riis in *How the Other Half Lives* had reported on poverty in the overcrowded and unsanitary tenements of American cities and industrial towns. The 1882 invention of the trust had led to abuses, prompting public support of government regulation of monopolies and the passage in 1890 of the Sherman Antitrust Act. Labor resorted to often violent strikes and boycotts, such as the 1892 Homestead strike for higher wages at the Carnegie Steel Company. Two years later, the *New Blood* company approached Chicago, which was under martial law during the Pullman strike, through miles of burning freight cars.

The Capitol (1895). *The Capitol* also wrestles with topical

issues—the influence of industry and religion on legislation.
The villains in the play—a coal combination, which closes its
Pennsylvania mines when the colliers strike, and Carroll, the
combination's lobbyist—try to corner the coal market and keep
coal prices high. When a newly reelected Nebraska representative, Will Blake, presents a resolution for duty-free raw materials, the lobbyist threatens to influence a committee vote against
Blake in his contested election and then offers him a bribe,
support for election to the Senate, if he will let his resolution
die in committee. The combination also buys out the only successful railroad carrier of Canadian coal to the United States
as added insurance if the resolution is adopted. After Blake
terminates his relations with moneyed interests, the combination
unsuccessfully uses money to defeat his election to the Senate
and then threatens to publish letters indicating his combination
ties unless he resigns his congressional seat.

The villains of industry are not alone in their unethical attempt
to influence legislation. When the only American cardinal, a
papal legate, resides in Baltimore, only one-half hour from
Washington, the Catholic church must have similar designs, in-
fers Judge Garrettson, Thomas's spokesman for the constitutional separation of church and state. Religious influence on
legislation is wrong, even though it might prevent poor families
from starving and dying of disease. The church instead should
provide charity to the oppressed and elevate public opinion.
It should support the election of just men, not men only of
its religious persuasion and definitely not men who feel obligated
to support the church's positions. The church might even use
the weapons of Wall Street to fight oppression by capital: in
the play the Catholic church influences a financier to call in
his loan to the combination, thus breaking the corner on the
nation's coal market and bankrupting it.

Besides their influence on legislation, the religious and political themes fit on another level: Blake and his wife, Agnes, are
an updated Adam and Eve, tempted by the Satan-like Carroll
in Washington, a promising but perilous Garden of Eden. Lured
by the idea of service to his country, Blake is too ambitious
of political ascendancy. Agnes dreams even of taking up residence in the White House.

Blake, somewhat naive and impulsive, is susceptible to manipulation. He not only succumbs to the temptation of political ascension at a cost to others, but also allows his wife to be exposed to Carroll's sexual advances because Carroll is an influential man in Washington. While Margaret Doane, head of the Royal Cross religious society, opens Blake's eyes to the dangers of Carroll, an unacquitted thief who seduced her into leaving her husband, Carroll tempts Agnes in the Blakes' own garden. Carroll tells her she has a responsibility to the men over whom she has an unconscious magnetic influence and reminds her of her social responsibility for Blake's political rise. She breaks from Carroll's attempted embrace as Blake steps into the garden. Blake's slapping of Carroll on the face signals the end of his relation with moneyed interests.

Blake is not immoral, but a malingerer. Regretful of his lapse, he is stronger because of his fall. In a world without perfect beings, he is a more dependable servant to his country than the unblemished politician who has never been tempted. He can be forgiven, and so can Margaret Doane, who provides charity to the oppressed and needy to atone for the wrong she did her husband and her daughter, Agnes, whom she left when the child was three years old.

This moral study of peculiarly American ambition provides an inside view of political life in Washington. Senator Whipple, in a comedy part, hurries to meet the Senate's first roll call so his attendance will be recorded in the newspapers of his home state, Tennessee. Ten minutes later he leaves the Senate chambers. On the eve of his reelection, he bemoans the political repercussions of his daughter's engagement to Wetmore-Boyd, a Catholic. He votes against duty-free raw materials to please, he thinks, his constituents, for Tennessee has undeveloped mines. When this vote and his support of Wetmore-Boyd's confirmation as ambassador to Italy prove politically unpopular, his public relations agents plan to lie his way out of the difficulty. They also plan to practice logrolling, for Tennessee's river counties, recently flooded, need federal assistance.

The influence of money is behind most political compromises in *The Capitol* (as a word, perhaps a pun). The combine pressures Blake. The chair of the House Committee on Contested Elections plans to rule against Blake's reelection, because of the money the former has invested in the coal combination. Carroll

advises Blake to camouflage his congressional representation
of the Anthracite Railroad by joining the Catholic church and
seeming to represent its interests. Political corruption by money
is so widespread that the president's appointment of Wetmore-
Boyd—made because of the country's need, with an active anti-
Catholic movement in the Midwest, for an ambassador with
whom the pope can readily confer—can be discredited by the
opposition party's charge of bargain and sale.

Counterbalancing this picture of political corruption are Wetmore-Boyd—who refuses to accept his confirmation because the
false charges against him will hurt his party's welfare—and the
recovered Blake—who plans to resign his Senate seat when
he initially thinks the combine's influence was responsible for
his election. Blake decides to stay in the Senate only after he
learns that the Catholic church, instrumental in his election,
attaches no obligations except that he be just.

Included in Thomas's portraits of Washington life is the role
of social life in political advancement. The Blakes take a house
on the exclusive Circle, and Mrs. Blake hosts receptions. The
political stock of her tea in act 3 is raised by the attendance
of distinguished guests like Father Eustace and Garrettson, who
reads a paper, but hurt by the absence of wives of the diplomatic
and cabinet circles. Blake is better known as Agnes's husband,
says Carroll, than as a tariff reformer. Her acquaintance with
Malcolm, one of the governing board members of the Cosmo-
politan Club, initially prevents Blake's being blackballed from
membership. Her later refusal of Malcolm's invitation to her,
but not to her husband, to sail the Potomac River with some
diplomats results in the board's decision against Blake.

The sketches of Washington political and social life are filled
with local color, such as the reception flowers loaned congressional wives by the federal government and Blake's detachable
shirt-sleeve cuffs, which are unfashionable. Much material is
topical, ranging from Italy's inefficient government to cigars
smuggled duty-free into the country and from the 1890s bicycling craze to Washington's black population. Senator Whipple
and his daughter, Cherry, ride bicycles on the stage, the former
for dyspepsia; a messenger slowly crosses the stage between
an exit and entrance reading a paperback novel by his bike
light. A Negro policeman walks across the stage, and a black

waiter, who brings sherbet and iced coffee, can quickly recognize southern "gentlemen" because they always call him "boy." The more important topical allusions are directly related to the play's themes. Blake's resolution alludes to the 1893–94 Wilson tariff bill, which was introduced to reduce the high tariff rates of the 1890 McKinley Act. Senators, charged by the press with representing special interests for campaign contributions, amended the Wilson bill several hundred times, restoring most of the high tariffs of the McKinley bill. The striking miners and their starving families allude to the violent strikes in Pennsylvania, Tennessee, Wyoming, and Idaho in 1892 and probably to the strike of 136 miners at Columbus, Ohio, in 1894. The Catholic presence in the play mirrors anti-Catholic sentiment, which reached a peak in the 1890s, particularly in the Midwest. The link between big business and legislation reflects the movement for direct election of senators, which began in the 1890s and resulted in the Seventeenth Amendment (1913), which ended the selection of senators by state legislatures.

In *The Capitol,* as in *New Blood,* Thomas tried to touch the country's heartbeat and interpret important national issues—the influence of special interests and religion on national legislation. *The Capitol* is in some ways a sequel to *New Blood,* showing the probable repercussions for laborers and national legislation if the farm equipment trust in the latter had been formed. Whereas *New Blood* says labor should not interfere with the trusts' promotion of tariffs and fixing of prices, *The Capitol* adds that Congress should. Labor unions, says Kerwin, have the right to strike for higher wages and better living conditions; capital, says *The Capitol,* should not close its facilities to break strikes.

Minor Plays

Thomas's interest as a playwright in socioeconomic and political issues is evident as early as the unproduced *Pittsburgh,* written in the early 1880s but probably revised later. Besides staging numerous violent scenes from the 1877 nationwide railroad strike, the play dramatizes strategy in the capital-labor confrontation. Management plans to gain support by agreeing to the workers' requests at the eleventh hour, when the laborers are so heated they will strike anyway. *The Spinner,* a talky one-act play unfavorably received at the Lambs Club in 1911, documents and criticizes the abuses of machine production during the industrialization of America. Craftsmen have become assembly-line workers. Women who once spun thread are now idle. And wealth is concentrated in the hands of machine owners.

The unproduced *The Mule Shoe,* a remodeling of *The Northwest,* probably in the early 1890s, depicts the struggle by thousands of water-turned stone mills to survive after 1882, when Minneapolis became the country's milling center. The play also indicts the Minneapolis mills' marketing practices. Distributing flour below cost, the mills try to corner the market so they can raise flour prices and lower employee wages. Two plays criticize trust practices. In the unproduced *The Gentleman from Texas,* which existed probably in several versions from the early 1890s to the early 1900s, a cotton trust tries to get a controlling interest in the invention of the round cotton bail to suppress its production. It then tries to deadlock a nominating convention for a House of Representatives race and influence the election by intimidating black voters. *The Member from Ozark* (Detroit, 1910) exposes methods by which a trust can attempt to influence legislation which would allow it to take by eminent domain Missouri's most valuable mineral land. To get a railroad bill passed, a national petroleum trust resorts to sexual and financial bribes and political pressure. A beautiful lady lobbyist, Stella Carmody, makes eyes at Deshna Poultney, a newly elected Missouri representative, and induces him to introduce the bill. Missouri state Senator Barton, an experienced politician, knows he has been bribed when his poker hand is called while he is holding four aces, his opponent has not even a pair, and two thousand dollars is on the table. He steers the trust-supported bill through the Senate. When Governor Holt decides not to support the railroad bill, the trust, which had offered money to ensure his election to the Senate if he will support its proposed tariff schedule, tries to defeat his election and prompts Barton to shoot him.

The Member from Ozark, using sixty speaking parts, also stages the balloting of a joint session of the Missouri Legislature. The clerk calls the roll as a brass band plays too loudly. The speaker pounds with a gavel, and cuspidors are rattled with the announcement of votes cast. Parliamentary jousting is shown: a point of order is raised and ruled as not debatable by the speaker, an attempt to go on record is ruled out of order, and a question of privilege is stated. A move to recess is defeated; a second move to recess passes. To force the governor to sign the railroad bill and elect certain persons to its commission of appraisers, the Legislature is thrown into a deadlock on its first nine ballots to elect a United States senator.

The political and economic themes of *The Member from Ozark* and *The Gentleman from Texas,* partially as a result of the popular and critical rejection of *New Blood* and *The Capitol,* were sacrificed to local color and conventional melodramatic plots. *Still Waters* (1926) instead failed because it is too much an editorial for the repeal of the Eighteenth Amendment. Besides demoralizing the young and breeding general disrespect for the law, Prohibition, says Thomas, leads to increased crime, encourages censorship, and violates personal and states' rights. Enforcement of national Prohibition is nearly impossible, he adds, wasting yearly millions of dollars, the equivalent of one-third of the annual national expenses.

Thomas and the Issues

Thomas's interest as a playwright in socioeconomic and political issues extends from the early 1880s through 1926. In addition to incidental criticism in numerous plays, four of his produced plays, three unproduced ones, and a playlet performed at the Lambs Club take a stand on contemporary issues. Labor, according to his plays, has the right to strike. Trusts lay off workers and raise prices, try to eliminate or absorb competition, and interfere with legislation. The need for direct election of senators is implied. Thomas's commentary is often associated with identifiable events, such as the 1877 nationwide strike, the 1892–94 strikes, the passage of the Wilson Tariff Act, and Prohibition.

The root of all these political and socioeconomic evils, except for sectarian influence on legislation, is the abuse of money. Thomas criticizes the inequitable distribution of the nation's riches, reflected in the poverty and disease of working-class families, the frivolous use of money by the newly rich, and the callous use of money by capitalists in business and politics. His call for the stewardship of money, a lack of class distinctions and special privileges, and equal opportunity for all precedes by more than three decades the next American play to advocate alternatives to the country's political and socioeconomic systems.

Chapter Five

Comedies

Thomas's comedies are his most enjoyable plays to present-day readers. His invigorating choice of situations and their quick and unexpected development transcend his use of standard farce-comedy devices, such as mistaken identities, coincidence, and embarrassing mix-ups. Characterization is subordinated to or blended with the fast pace and unexpected turns in direction. Reader interest is focused on the attempt at extrication that inevitably leads to further complication.

These plays are polished models of construction and technique, indebted to Thomas's exposure to the experimentation in little theaters in Paris during his 1902–5 residency in France. They are contemporaneous and American in subject matter. Even *The Earl of Pawtucket,* about an Englishman who courts an American heiress, derives its humor from the earl's attempt to be ultra-American.

Major Plays

Thomas began his farce-comedy period, from 1899 through 1906, with his least characteristic play, a costume comedy of manners about a man and literary circle known in anecdote and biography. Sketching with epigrams and sayings associated with the Samuel Johnson literary circle, Thomas in *Oliver Goldsmith* (1900) creates a portrait gallery of eighteenth-century notables: Boswell, constantly taking notes for his *Life of Johnson;* Johnson, rugged on the exterior but gentle within; Garrick, an actor off stage, mimicking, for example, Johnson's pronunciation of "punch" as "poonsh" and playing countless practical jokes; and Goldsmith, too modest to express his love for Mary Horneck. Though Thomas researched the lives and writings of the Johnson coterie, his play is not based on research alone. The depiction of the coffeehouse atmosphere of that circle owes much to Thomas's experience and observation of the camaraderie at the Lambs Club.

Avoiding the temptation to tell many of the attractive incidents in Goldsmith's biography, Thomas treated instead the conception of *She Stoops to Conquer,* Goldsmith's mistaking a private home for an inn (act 1), its rehearsal (act 2), and the immediate consequences of its success (act 3). He makes the critic Kenrick Goldsmith's rival for Mary Horneck and ends the second act, in which a scene from *She Stoops to Conquer* is burlesqued, with the playwright's caning of Kenrick. Act 3 implies the promise of a marriage between Goldsmith and Horneck. The love interest, the weakest motif in the play and the dominant concern of act 3, may have been played down in the drama because Stuart Robson, who acted the part of Goldsmith, was more effective in comedy roles than in serious ones.

In *On the Quiet* (1901), Thomas begins to use effectively the trademark of his major farce comedies—complication followed by extrication. In act 1, Robert Ridgway, in love with Agnes Colt, agrees not to see Agnes during his matriculation at college to satisfy her brother, who wants his sister to marry a nobleman and has the right by stipulation of will to reduce her dowry by sixteen million dollars if she marries without his consent. In the second act, when Agnes and several of her friends arrive unexpectedly at Ridgway's Yale University quarters, where two music-hall girls are present, Ridgway inventively directs traffic rushing in and out of doors and windows. Then he escapes from the compromising situation by sailing with Agnes and her friends into a fog. In the fourth act, amid the continuation of farcical incidents, Agnes's brother comes to the yacht via tugboat and, learning of Robert and Agnes's earlier matrimony, consents to the marriage. The runaway match becomes a honeymoon cruise.

As in *Surrender,* Thomas uses a surplus of characters, but he ingeniously moves the eighteen characters about so that no one lingers uselessly. And, unlike *Colorado,* the play focuses: the hero always stays effortlessly in the center of the picture.

In *The Earl of Pawtucket* (1903), an English earl and an American divorcée momentarily encounter each other three times on the Continent; each becomes attracted to the other without knowledge of the other's rank or financial worth. The earl,

Lord Cardington, crosses the Atlantic Ocean to court Harriet
Fordyce, who has resumed her birth name. He experiences a
series of complications, because Harriet's ex-husband, Mont-
gomery Putnam, a practical joker, persuades the earl to assume
his name and equips the Englishman with his own luggage and
an address book of relatives and friends. The earl meets several
Putnam family members whose names he cannot keep separated
in his mind. He is forced to pay Putnam's alimony and is begged
to consent to marriages of a Putnam sister and niece. Another
Putnam sister accuses the earl of stealing her brother's trunk;
because Putnam is missing and his clothing is in the trunk, the
earl is nearly arrested for murder.

As in *On the Quiet,* Thomas ingeniously constructs complications and rapidly develops a tightly structured play with unity
of time and place. The play's three scenes during the morning,
noon, and afternoon of the same day take place in the parlor
and in the Palm and Turkish Coffee rooms of the Waldorf-
Astoria. The depiction of Lord Cardington transcends the carica-
ture of the silly Englishman typical on the American stage, as
did the similar characterizations of Lord Dundreary in Tom
Taylor's *Our American Cousin* (1858) and Lord Chumley in David Belasco and Henry C. De Mille's play of the same name
(1888).

The earl's part was written for Lawrence D'Orsay, a minor
actor and refined Englishman, whose discourse and manners
amused Americans most when he was trying to be ultra-American. Charles Frohman, who had commissioned the play, liked
The Earl of Pawtucket, but refused to risk its production with
D'Orsay in the leading role. Renowned for his ability to pick
box-office successes, Frohman again demonstrated his uncanny
knack of letting Thomas's big fish, like *Arizona* and *The Witching
Hour,* get away. The play, quickly grabbed for production by
Kirk La Shelle, ran for 191 performances in New York and
was performed in London in 1907. D'Orsay starred in *The Earl
of Pawtucket* for three years, and in later years he toured the
country with it.

In *The Other Girl* (1903)—titled "The Pug and the Parson"
until a couple of Protestant ministers objected—world-champion
middleweight boxer Kid Garvey under an assumed name is
hired to train Reverend Bradford in fighting. An engaged soci-

ety girl, Catherine, spies the two wrestling and, imagining she
is in love with Garvey, plans to elope with him via automobile.
Her adopted "sister," Estelle, locks Catherine in the garden,
however, and disguised by a car mask, takes Catherine's place
in the elopement. Thomas now piles complication upon complication, all occurring between eight P.M. and eight A.M. on a
June night. The parson leaps from a second-story window to
rescue Catherine, who is kicking in the locked stained-glass doors
leading from the garden. He has to use Garvey's wrestling techniques on the butler, who is convinced that the minister is the
cause of Catherine's rage. Garvey and Estelle run down Reginald
Lumley, Catherine's fiance, and are locked up at the police station. Estelle, who has Catherine's jewels and luggage, is sus-
pected of robbery. Complications are quickly unentangled, and
all ends well with Catherine, the girl men come to look at,
realizing she loves Lumley, and Estelle, the other girl, the one
men stay to talk with, accepting the minister's proposal.

For the role of Kid Garvey, Lionel Barrymore imitated the
mannerisms and ring vernacular of Kid McCoy, at that time
the world-champion middleweight boxer; before each performance he even curled his hair so it resembled the fighter's hair
style. The play ran for 160 nights in New York before being
taken on a western tour.

Whereas *Oliver Goldsmith* was inspired by actor Stuart Robson's resemblance to the profile portraits of Oliver Goldsmith
and *The Earl of Pawtucket* by Lawrence D'Orsay's personality,
habits of thought, and mannerisms of speech, *Mrs. Leffingwell's
Boots* (1905) germinated from odds and ends and remnants: a
dinner party the Thomases gave during a snowstorm, at which
only one of ten guests arrived; and a dinner table fountain that
spurted eccentrically one night when Francis Wilson was narrat-
ing a story, streaming onto the bosom of his dress shirt. In
Mrs. Leffingwell's Boots, the worst snowstorm "since Roscoe
Conklin died" isolates in the Bonners' suburban New York
home Mabel Ainslee, a house guest for whom a dinner party
has been arranged; Walter Corbin, a young architect driven
into the home to make a telephone call and detained by the
matchmaking hostess; and Mrs. Leffingwell. Corbin and Mabel,
whose engagement had been broken when a woman's boots
on the fire escape outside of his Bar Harbor hotel room had

led to talk, reconcile. Then complications arise. Mabel finds out that Mrs. Leffingwell is the woman of the scandal. Mr. Leffingwell, who had kicked in the door to Corbin's hotel room, hastens into the storm and toward the Bonners' when he learns that his wife and Corbin are in proximity in their bedroom attire. Corbin and Dr. Rumsey, the Bonners' father-in-law, apprehend a burglar and gag him with Mrs. Leffingwell's boots. A manikin posing as the burglar is guarded with a candle disguised as a gun, and an eccentric dinner table water fountain sprays the butler on the chest. Other humorous incidents briskly chase one another before jealous suspicions are put to rest and Dr. Rumsey practices osteopathy to cure the burglar, Mabel's brother, who—morally deranged since a blow in a schoolboy fight left pressure on a nerve—had planted Mrs. Leffingwell's boots outside Corbin's hotel room.

Minor Comedies

Besides his farce-comedies, Thomas wrote several comedies, none of which is crucial. *Combustion* (1884), the revised *For Money* (1891), the one-act *The Man Upstairs* (1895), and *The Meddler* (1898) foreshadow Thomas's major farces. *Surrender* (1892) and *Colonel Carter of Cartersville* (1892) were written to cash in on the interest in the South, heightened by the success of *Alabama. Champagne Charlie* (1901) is an inferior musical comedy. *The Education of Mr. Pipp* (1905) dramatizes cartoons by Charles Dana Gibson. *DeLancey* (1905) and *The Embassy Ball* (1906), written at the end of Thomas's farce-comedy period and shortly before the appearance of his theme plays, shows Thomas's waning interest in farce-comedy.

The nonextant *Combustion,* written with Edgar Smith for the Dickson Sketch Club, was a hodgepodge of comical situations, songs, and burlesque. Though lacking the tight structure of Thomas's later farce-comedies, it shows Thomas's predisposition to farce and to comedy, which appears in all his plays. *For Money* is Thomas's collaboration with Clay M. Greene for actor William Crane, who created memorable American characters in *The Senator* (1889) and *The Governor of Kentucky* (1896). Crane, whose talent was in comedy, wanted a play that was basically serious, but when the opening performance of *For Money* elicited laughter at the wrong times, Thomas quickly revised the story of a man embittered by finding in his dead wife's locket a picture of another man into a comical character sketch of businessman Winfield Farragut Curney, a yacht club commodore afraid to go to sea and a militia colonel who has never fired a gun. Against the protests of women more sporting than he, Gurney, as the commodore, delays the Larchmont Yacht Club race under the pretext of choppy waves. As a capitalist, he stages a bogus strike of the Surcingle Electric Railroad, of which he is a president, to depress its securities and thereby test the sincerity of his daughter's suitors, the loyalty of his friends, and the love of a widow. When an actual strike results, the colonel is ordered to put down mob rule. He mounts a horse on stage and leads his militia boldly forth, but only after the widow's chiding and his having bought off the strike. The clever complications and incessant movement, particularly of the energetic but timid Gurney, foreshadow techniques effectively used by Thomas in his farce-comedies of the early 1900s.

Colonel Carter of Cartersville, more episodic than *Alabama,* is Thomas's adaptation of Francis Hopkinson Smith's novel of the same name. Besides the slightly developed addition of Colonel Carter's love interest for a young ward, absent during two acts, Thomas closely followed the original in characterization, incidents, dialogue, and atmosphere.

Carter quixotically cherishes a scheme of engineering a railroad through his garden state of Virginia to the sea, but he lacks capital and, considering mortgage payments as mere legal technicalities, barely avoids foreclosure on the Carter Hall mansion. In New York, where he travels to raise capital for his visionary venture, he imagines a Wall Street broker's correct appraisal of the Carter collateral to be a personal insult necessitating a duel; and he lives opulently on credit, which he understands not as a financial obligation, but as a gift, a sign of the new era of good feeling between the North and South.

Besides the portrait of Carter, Thomas creates three original American stage characters: Carter's Negro servant Chad; the broker, so much the practical New York businessman he is unaware that gentlemen exist; and a grocer, so disarmed by the Colonel's hospitality and effusive compliments when he arrives to collect for two months of bills that he leaves unpaid and eager to provide Carter, free of charge, his entire stock of Madeira wine. Chad, except for fiddling for dancing black children and quarreling with his wife in act 1, is not the conventional Negro servant. This wise and affectionate butler at times fathers Carter, at times becomes exasperated with his unworldliness, but is always devoted to him.

Surrender, unlike traditional Civil War plays such as Bronson Howard's *Shenandoah* (1889) and William Gillette's *Held by the Enemy* (1886), has no battle scenes with firing of guns and roaring of cannons, no prison scenes with picturesque types and the attempted execution of a spy prevented at the last moment. Though the scenes are set in and near besieged Richmond in 1865, the only visible evidence of a violent war are privations, such as tattered southern uniforms, scant meals, and the use of wash blue for ink, and two war events—the escape of one hundred Union soldiers from Libby prison and the foiling of the southern attempt to free Confederate prisoners at Lake Erie's Johnson Island and subsequent march on New York. Both of these war events are in the background and are not staged. As in *Reckless Temple, Alabama,* and later in *New Blood, The Capitol,* and *The Witching Hour,* Thomas was departing from set dramatic forms and traditions. Believing the Civil War was far enough in the past to be treated comically, he presented the quieter social, amiable, and humorous aspects of the conflict. There are no villains and no attribution of sentiment less honorable to one side than the other. Union prisoners in love with the three daughters of Confederate General Colgate, better able to manage his troops than his household, are invited to a ball at his Richmond home and aided by the daughters in conveying to Abraham Lincoln the southern plans for liberating the Confederates on Johnson Island.

Charles Frohman, whose first big hit was *Shenandoah* and who had a predilection for the traditional war play, produced *Surrender* seriously, melodramatizing the incidents and even introducing a horse. The mixture of the comical and the seriously melodramatic made the play seem irreverent to the South and led audience and critics alike to look for improbabilities. Accordingly, the play ran for a month in Boston and lasted only sixteen weeks on the road, with Charles Frohman taking a loss of $28,000.

The Man Upstairs is a comedy of situation, in which the man from upstairs returns from a business trip and mistakes for his own a flat on a lower floor of the apartment building. He unpacks his valise, makes himself comfortable, and wonders about the changes his wife has made in the apartment during his absence. The wife of the couple who owns the apartment arrives, then the husband, and finally the wife from upstairs, creating jealous misunderstandings. The curtain falls with all parties talking and gesticulating at the same time.

In *The Meddler* (1898), Frank Eli imagines that Mrs. Bancroft, a young wife of a friend, is intimate with the ladies' man Frank Chandler. His comical attempt to save the marriage of his jealous friend, filled with sidestepping, lying, and blundering, leads to a series of complications in which two married and two engaged couples are all embroiled in accusations and misunderstandings.

In *The Education of Mr. Pipp,* the slight-of-figure Mr. Pipp, a nouveau industrial millionaire seeming to deserve continuous coddling, is besieged in the parlor of his New York home by a stout domineering wife. He agrees to travel abroad to escape his wife's charges and to indulge his two beautiful daughters, who are mirror images of the 1890s Gibson girl. From Mr. Pipp's arranging of encounters between his daughter Julia and an English riding master through his fisticuffing the counterfeit count serving as their European guide, events on the lawn of Lady Fitzmaurice's Carony Castle in England and New York and a crowded Paris hotel closely follow incidents in Gibson's cartoons. The play, like Gibson's drawings, portrays both sides of the issue of heiress-nobility marriages: the riding master, who turns out to be Lady Fitzmaurice's son, a lord, gets one daughter; the distinctly American manager of Pipp's Pittsburgh Iron Works gets the other.

The character of the protagonist in *DeLancey* grew from Thomas's association with a dinner host who hired an artist to touch up a picture he could not afford to replace so that his divorced wife would not be recognizable in it. DeLancey, a divorced bachelor fond of fox hunting, is financially supported by only Aunt Ruth's and Dr. Morton's yearly dole of two thousand dollars each. He receives permission to marry his childhood friend Jacqui only after he resolves to support himself by training Japanese horsemen. The love interest in the play is not engaging;

and the play capitalizes on current fads like fox hunting and phrenology.

Originally, *The Embassy Ball* was a four-act comedy with serious elements: during Panama's revolution against Columbia, diplomats in Washington make fateful decisions; United States gunboats and the *H.M.S. Renown* nearly combat; and speculation in Panama rubber trees, valuable because of the rising car industry, affects national political decisions. When D'Orsay proved unsatisfactory in a semi-serious leading role, Thomas revised the play as a three-act farce without allusion to the Panama conflict. Though the play had only forty-eight performances in New York, it ran for two years on the road.

Though Thomas's comedies and farce-comedies are entertaining, they have little lasting value. They are contemporaneous and American in subject matter, but, except for their cleverness in construction and wittiness in dialogue, they did not improve American drama.

Chapter Six

Psychological and Psychic Plays

The Witching Hour, The Harvest Moon, and *As a Man Thinks* dramatize many of Thomas's psychological and psychic theories of the powers, faculties, and characteristics of the conscious and subconscious minds. *The Witching Hour* presents his view of the dynamic nature of thought as witnessed through the phenomena of telepathy and hypnotism, and the law of suggestion; *The Harvest Moon* studies further the law of suggestion and analyzes a personality disorder; and *As a Man Thinks* explores his thought about the sexual double standard and the relationship of health and emotion.

Much of Thomas's thought in his supernormal and pathological plays challenges typical concepts of time, space, matter, and logic; but his thought is based on a comprehensive and systematic theory of the subconscious mind developed in part from scrutiny of the literature of dynamic psychology and psychical research, as well as biology, medicine, and physics. Thomas's conclusions, however, are never bookish, but backed by firsthand observation and investigation, occasionally with acknowledged authorities in these scientific fields.

His psychological and psychical studies—the first serious American plays based on the scientific findings of abnormal psychology and psychical research—are major events in the history of American drama and theater. They helped widen the stage to include serious thematic plays, a development essential for the rise of modern American drama. The box-office successes of *The Witching Hour* (in 1907, 212 performances in New York, with concurrent production by a company in Chicago) and *As a Man Thinks* (in 1911, 128 performances in New York) also helped convince theater managers that idea plays might be profitable and ushered in a psychic period upon the American stage.

Formative Influences

The Thomas family's attitude toward psychic phenomena created an atmosphere conducive to a cultivation of interest in paranormal processes. Though his father was agnostic about spiritistic claims, his mother's agnosticism was encompassed by an atmosphere of belief; and his maternal grandmother claimed to be able to communicate with spirits, thereby prescribing on at least six occasions successful remedies for family illnesses that puzzled doctors.

The most profound early catalyst for Thomas's inquiry into the nature of the subconscious mind, however, was his experience in 1889 as press agent for the American-born mind reader Washington Irving Bishop. Bishop (c. 1848–89) became a famous exposer of spiritualist mediums and clairvoyants by demonstrating how their feats could be accomplished through deception, contortionist maneuvers, and mind reading. He toured America in 1877 and then England, where he attracted extensive attention in 1878 and 1881, performing before the Prince of Wales, as well as fashionable people of society and prominent scientists, including Thomas Huxley. After 1882 he gave demonstrations before many of the crowned rulers of Europe. In 1889, when Bishop returned to America, Thomas, who had recently resigned as a business manager for the Marlowe Company touring the United States, became Bishop's advance man, making the arrangements for his public exhibitions.

During this brief employment, Thomas witnessed Bishop finding "while blind-folded, hidden articles; playing melodies mentally suggested by other persons; locating some chosen word in a large library of books; driving blind-folded a team of horses through the city streets."[1] On May 12, 1889, however, Bishop suffered several cataleptic fits and became unconscious after performing at a Lambs Club gambol in New York City. Though it was common knowledge that Bishop had repeatedly suffered from cataleptic trances in which he appeared to be dead, a too hasty autopsy was performed by a coroner and the New York Hospital's pathologist.

Some accused Bishop of fraud and/or shrewd interpretations of signals unconsciously transmitted by his subjects, as in muscle reading, in which the mind reader interprets the nearly imper-

ceptible and involuntary movements of tension and relaxation
of a subject thinking of the actualization of a certain willed
activity. But Thomas believed in the authenticity of Bishop's
performances. He repeatedly testified in speeches, interviews,
and print to the importance of Bishop's message of the dynamic
nature of thought. He also wrote and distributed a small pam-
phlet titled "Personal Experiences with a Clairvoyant."

Thomas knew other psychics, one of whom, he said, was superior to Bishop, possessing the dynamic, as well as the receptive,
side of telepathy. Thomas was also an acquaintance and friend
of leading psychical researchers. He knew Pierre Janet, the
French psychologist, whom he probably first met during his
1902–5 residency in France, and James Hyslop, the president
from 1906 to 1920 of the American Society for Psychical Research. The latter, with whom Thomas talked extensively, re-
quested him to publish his personal observations on psychic
phenomena. Robert Wood—a noted physicist, who with others
had investigated the Neapolitan medium Eusapia Paladion—
was a friend and neighbor at Thomas's East Hampton, New
York, home. And Hamlin Garland, an exacting investigator
of spiritism, was also a close friend. In a letter sent to Lisle
Colby on Thomas's death, Garland hoped "for a message from
him in some way for we were both students and experimenters
in psychic matters."[2]

Besides having several psychic experiences, mainly accurate
impressions of trouble threatening relatives, Thomas read the
principal writers and works on psychic phenomena, including
William James, James Hervey Hyslop, Thomas Jay Hudson,
and the publications of the English Society for Psychical Research and its American counterpart.[3] He was familiar with the
historical development of supernormal phenomena from the end
of the eighteenth century on and with paranormal cognition
(knowledge gained by other than sensory means), paranormal
physical phenomena (phenomena produced by an individual
independently of the body's motor system), and paranormal
subconscious processes. He viewed these phenomena not as iso-
lated occurrences but as varying manifestations of the same or
similar psychic laws. Being rational in his approach, he based
his explanations not on supernatural causation but on known
physical and unknown superphysical agencies. The concept by

which Thomas accounted for diverse paranormal phenomena—
such as hypnotism, faith cures, discarnate voices, apparitions,
automatic writing, multiple personality, insanity, dreams, and
spontaneous solutions to different problems—was that of the
subconscious mind. This concept underlies his psychological and
psychic plays, as well as his dramatic theories.

Major Plays

The Witching Hour (1907). After manager A. M. Palmer
in 1890 had rejected the one-act *A Constitutional Point* as being
too abstruse in theme, Thomas continued to collect from his
personal experiences and reading material for a psychic drama.
Gradually the playlet developed in his mind into *The Witching
Hour,* of which *A Constitutional Point* became with minor changes
act 2.

In the first act of the play, set at Brookfield's gambling house
in Louisville, twenty-year-old Clay Whipple, a promising architect with a compulsive fear of cat's-eyes, accidentally kills a man
taunting him with such a gem; and the assistant district attorney,
Frank Hardmuth, in love with Clay's sweetheart, Viola, prose-
cutes him for personal, as well as professional, reasons. Clay
is convicted of murder, and the case is appealed to the Supreme
Court on the grounds that trial attendance was restricted to
those favorable to the prosecution. Clay's mother, Helen Whipple, visits Justice Prentice in Washington, asking him to read
a letter he had written during his early manhood to her mother,
Margaret Price. The letter concerns a duel he had fought with
a man who had taunted Prentice's sweetheart, Margaret, with
a cat's-eye; Clay's homicide resulted from a seemingly inherited
hysteria.

A new trial begins. In the seclusion of his library, Brookfield,
Viola's uncle, concentrates his attention on one juror possibly
friendly to the defense. He also enlists against Hardmuth the
minds of 500,000 newspaper readers sympathetic to his printed
charge that Hardmuth had planned to kill the Kentucky gover-
nor-elect. Public thought evidently influences the sequestered
jury. Clay is acquitted. Hardmuth rushes in to Brookfield's library and thrusts a derringer against Brookfield's chest; staring

him in the eyes, the gambler tells the district attorney that he
cannot fire the gun, and dominated by Brookfield's will, the
incredulous Hardmuth drops it. Later, Brookfield, convinced
he may have transmitted by thought the murder plan to the
assistant district attorney, transports Hardmuth across the river
to Indiana and safety from the manhunt triggered by his accusation. The play also illustrates the mechanics of paranormal cognition and includes in act 2 one of the most effective dramatic
scenes Thomas ever constructed, a convincing suggestion of
the presence of Margaret's spirit and her communication with
the living in Prentice's library-living room.

In the play, Jack Brookfield, a gentleman gambler and collector of fine paintings, becomes aware of his psychic ability and
the play's two themes, one the moral application of the other:
thought is dynamic; individuals, therefore, are responsible for
the moral quality of their thoughts as well as their deeds. Jack
had possessed paranormal powers before the beginning of the
play, as indicated by his luck at gambling. When young, he
had healed through mesmerism (along with "animal magnetism," an early label for hypnotism), but had discontinued public
demonstrations after entering local politics. He also had telepathically influenced Helen Whipple, who later rejected his marriage
proposal because of his profession, often to rise from sleep while
in college and write him a letter.

In act 1, Supreme Court Justice Prentice visits Jack Brookfield's home and gambling establishment, admiring the Corot
he cannot afford to buy. Through this meeting, Brookfield becomes aware of his own "strong, hypnotic power."[4] Prentice
correctly surmises that Brookfield's friends often had introduced
independent subjects about which he was intending to speak
and that Brookfield had shut out the likely truth—that his apparent thought was not his own but that of his friend. Reading
two books on psychic phenomena that Prentice mails to him,
Jack begins to experiment with hypnosis and clairvoyance. By
act 2 his power has increased. He has put a man to sleep with
a half dozen mesmeric passes and induced hypnotic sleep in a
person who had then seen what a boy (Clay Whipple) was doing
a mile away in jail.

After this meeting with Prentice, Jack's psychic investigation
continues. In act 2 he reveals to Helen some experiments involv-

ing her, of which she had not been aware: a month before he had caused her to knock on his door at two in the morning and ask if he were ill, and later he had influenced her to walk to a church door, hesitate, and then return home. During this act he remains at home while the jury is deliberating, convinced that by thought he can sway the decision of one juror. Evidently he does influence that juror, leading him to ask a question about possible verdicts during the judge's instructions to the jury. By having the charge against Hardmuth printed, he also influences the jury through the psychic transmission of public opinion. Jack's other demonstration of psychic power in the third act occurs when Hardmuth rushes into Jack's library and presses a derringer against him. Turning on an electric lamp above and just in front of Hardmuth's eyes, Jack asserts, "You can't shoot—that—gun." Confronted by the eyes of Jack and Prentice, *"a double battery of hypnotism"* (91), Hardmuth helplessly drops the gun.

In act 4 Jack performs his last telepathic feat in the play. He gazes in the fire, thus inducing a state of semi-autohypnosis, while Lew Ellinger, a family friend, shuffles and deals a hand of draw. Then Jack shocks Lew by telling him that he (Lew) is holding three queens. Directing Lew to draw one card from the deck, Jack correctly identifies the selected card as the ace of hearts.

Whereas Jack develops in psychic understanding and expression and mature moral sensibility, Prentice is a static character, the psychic ideal or standard toward which Jack evolves. As such, he is the stationary backdrop against which Jack's level and rate of psychic progress can be measured.

In addition to being the character destination toward which Jack is journeying, Prentice is Jack's psychic mentor. He is familiar with scientifically conducted psychical research, its implications and literature. He is motivated by altruistic instincts and is known for his charity. He is disinclined to persuade Jack to reduce the selling price of a Corot painting by appealing to Jack's weakness for sentiment. Prentice also is psychically endowed. In act 1 he knows that Jack can be swayed by an appeal to sentiment, that the price for the Corot is $6,500, and that Jack in his mind is questioning the location of Prentice's residence. To highlight Jack's psychic progress in the play, Thomas

after the first act sketches only two of Prentice's psychic feats:
he awakens a friend by thought at two in the morning and
influences him to call the telepathist, and he relieves Jack's headache by thought.

By dramatizing the theory of "non-accidental coincidence,"
Thomas further develops his theme of the dynamic nature of
thought. Seeming coincidences, according to Thomas, are often
due to telepathy between living or living and dead persons.
Prentice's awareness of Jack's unannounced visit and Jack and
Helen's writing to each other simultaneously are events that,
in spite of their apparently causeless nature, are attributable
to telepathy between living persons.

The numerous coincidences of act 2 are primarily attributable
to telepathy between the living and the deceased. Justice Prentice tells Justice Henderson, with whom he is playing chess,
that he believes in only one way in that "Bret Harte stuff"
(the spiritism of Harte's "Newport Legend," which inspired
this act): as he gets older, the contents of his memory—such
as his boyhood companions—become more real every day, even
more tangible than they were in life. Later in the act, Helen
Whipple visits Prentice to plead for his favorable vote on an
appeal for a retrial of her son, convicted of murder. She brings
with her a letter from Prentice to her mother, Margaret Price,
and one of Margaret's handkerchiefs filled with the odor of
mignonette, of which she was fond. When Helen mentions Margaret's name shortly after the justice had spoken to Henderson
about his former sweetheart and her miniature had fallen to
the floor, Prentice wonders "if what we call coincidences are
ever mere coincidences" (68). Rounding out his sentence in
the manuscript of *A Constitutional Point* is the phrase "or the
result of some psychic force." Also deleted in the same manuscript, probably for being too explicit, is his reply of "Coincidence number three" when the pleading mother rhetorically
asks him, "Can you imagine my joy when I found the letter
was on the very point of this inherited trait on which we rested
our defense?"[5] At the end of the act, smelling the mignonette
from Margaret's handkerchief, he fancies not that his memory
is playing tricks on him but that he has been influenced from
the other side of the grave.

In addition to Jack's and Prentice's psychic feats and the theory of "non-accidental coincidence," Thomas dramatizes the dynamic nature of thought in Clay's aversion for the cat's-eye jewel, which caused him accidentally to kill a man, and in the correlation between visual thinking and success. As a result of his fear, Clay, a promising architect at the beginning of the play, is still as "weak as dishwater," too dependent upon his mother, too effeminate, and too much a boy. Clay's fear is due not to the jewel's occult power or to inherited insanity but to suggestion. Jack demonstrates that Clay's hysteria is founded on his mental attitude: holding a night key in his closed fist, Jack tells Clay that he has in his hand the jewel; Clay feels its influence tingling through and through him, down his back and at the roots of his hair. Disclosing his deception and using positive suggestion, Jack pins the cat's-eye jewel to Viola's breast, and Clay is able to embrace her without becoming hysterical.

Clay's ability visually to perceive a room in its three dimensions before he designs it hints that he will become a successful architect. His picturing Viola in the homes he designs also indicates that he, not Hardmuth, will win her hand. The often involuntary appearance of these images suggests that Clay has psychic powers.

Prentice also possesses the ability to visualize. In telepathically influencing a friend, he mentally pictures the person going to the telephone and calling. And in explaining the reason for the presence of past friends in his mind, he employs a visual analogy based on a Rousseau painting. The importance of visualization is further illustrated by the number of paintings seen or alluded to in the play as well as Clay's profession as architect.

The second theme of *The Witching Hour,* the responsibility of each individual for his thought, was expressed by Thomas in a curtain speech on the opening night of the play:

The members of a large part of the community with whom I am in sympathy have long been accustomed to regard their private minds as parks in which there might be neither prohibition nor policeman; but if, as scientists assert, a malignant and destructive thought of mine, like a circling Marconigram, affects, first my family, then friends, then acquaintances, before it finally filters impotently to its finish, I want to know it; and if, after twenty years of fairly intelligent investigation, I believe that it is so, I feel it my duty as a dramatist to state it.[6]

This theme is dramatized through Jack's development. At the beginning of the play, he is "negatively good," moral but not spiritual. Ostensibly he is honest; his customers receive a fair game. Discovering, however, that telepathy has played a hand in his gambling success, he gives up gambling. Realizing that "a guilty thought is almost as criminal as a guilty deed," he has also accepted responsibility for the Scovill murder. Thinking that Scovill deserved to be killed, Jack had imagined the same murder plan that Hardmuth had later followed in arranging Scovill's death. Being in rapport with Hardmuth, he thinks his ideas possibly had telepathically influenced Hardmuth to procure Scovill's death. Having developed spiritually as well as intellectually, Jack helps Hardmuth escape from arrest.

The themes of the play—that thought is dynamic and operates in a normal framework—are inseparable from the concept of a cosmic subjective mind informing reality. Jack's development in psychic power and moral character is due to his perception of this infinite mind, its laws, and providential character. Through gradually deepening insight, Jack discovers a philosophical law—that affective and, to a certain extent, sensory states are existential—and a moral-physical law—that thoughts and emotions are moral or immoral, and moral strength promotes physical strength and well-being.

Emotions, being existential, can be chosen, rejected, or controlled: an attitudinal change in state of mind can erase or intensify emotions. Thomas dramatizes this philosophical law in Jack's exorcism of Clay's fear of the cat's-eye jewel, simply a "notion" that an "effort of will can banish" (97), and in Clay's hatred of Hardmuth. Hatred is "weak-minded"; the "power that any man or anything has to annoy us we give him or it by our interest" (97). Physical sensations can also be a result of choice. Jack simply "thinks" he has a headache; Prentice cures him by "thinking" that Jack does not.

Discovery of this philosophical law leads Jack to stress courage as part of the code by which one should live. In facing Hardmuth, Clay begins to overcome his effeminate nature. In disarming, not repressing, her sense of guilt for Clay's homicide, Helen can transcend her hysteria concerning this accident.

The moral-physical law Jack gradually perceives states that the selfish or altruistic nature of emotions physically affects their generator. Emotions that are self-centered damage the transmitter more than the person at whom they are directed. Clay needs to learn to dismiss his hatred of Hardmuth, for "hatred is heavier freight for the shipper than . . . the consignee" (96).[7] Similarly, Jack's headache in act 1, which has intensified by act 2, and his "paler and less physical" appearance (62) in act 2 are due to his misuse or at least a nonmoral use of psychic ability. Psychic power, as Prentice explains to Jack, "opens to the investigator new mental heights, higher planes—and every man . . . is ill in some manner who lives habitually on a lower level—than the light he sees" (66).

In contrast to the enervating effect of selfish emotions, altruistic emotions improve physical health and increase physical strength, for the person becomes the medium of expression for the infinite mind. Thus Jack tells Clay that as a child of God, that is, expressing fully the infinite mind by embodying only altruistic impulses, he cannot be hurt. Jack's belief is dramatized in his preventing Hardmuth, motivated by selfish emotions, from shooting him.

The providential nature of the infinite mind is expressed in the neither accidentally nor telepathically produced coincidences in the play, for example, Clay's inspiration for the design of Jack's library and Helen's dropping of a paper cutter followed by Jack's walking to her to pick it up. The Corot painting, which inspires Clay's design, introduces Jack to Prentice, thus establishing a contact that affects the remanding of Clay's trial. The physical proximity of Helen and Jack, which is due to the fallen paper cutter, symbolizes the future intimacy of their relationship. The paper cutter, then placed by Jack on a table, becomes instrumental in Denning's death. The time Jack and Helen spend together as a result of Clay's trial cements their relationship and leads to their marriage. These events form part of an overall design in which creation progresses from selfishness to altruism, with man in the vanguard of that progress.

Psychic theories influenced not only the content of *The Witching Hour* but also the construction of plot and selection of dramatis personae, the appeal to instincts, the repetitive use of props, and the suggestive and symbolic use of setting and properties. In the play, for example, when Thomas adds the theme of the dynamic nature of thought to the theme of coincidence in *A*

Constitutional Point, he portrays Clay, affected negatively by suggestion, as passive and weak. To raise audience sympathy for
this somewhat unattractive person, Thomas appeals to the instinct of defense of kin in Helen's anxiety for her son and to
the instinct of reproduction in Viola's love for Clay. Dramatic
opposition to Clay, naturally available in the law, he personifies
in the character of the assistant district attorney Frank Hardmuth
and intensifies by making Hardmuth a suitor of Viola, further
appealing to the instinct of reproduction.

Thomas selected as the proponent of telepathy Justice Prentice
with his psychic ability and knowledgeable understanding of
psychic literature and research. Jack Brookfield, an art-loving
gambler who has unconsciously misused his psychic ability by
the beginning of the play and becomes aware of his telepathic
ability during it, becomes Prentice's opponent. Further appeal
to the instinct of reproduction is created by making Jack and
Helen former sweethearts and by having Jack court her. Addi-
tional appeal to the instinct of self-preservation, already present
in Clay's struggle for acquittal, is generated through Hardmuth's
attempted shooting of Jack. The spectator's doubt or disbelief
in the theme of the play is personified primarily by an "attorney
for the people," Lew Ellinger. Ellinger is comic, for to doubt
in the context of the play would be comic, but he is also good-
hearted and likable, for he represents the audience.

Thomas repetitively and effectively employs several props—
such as the cat's-eye jewel, the miniature, and the volume of
Bret Harte's poems—as accessories for the climactic moments
of the play. A prop is introduced before its climactic use. Before
the ivory tusk-shaped paper cutter is employed to kill Denning,
Thomas establishes its proper function when Viola, while gossip-
ing, cuts magazine leaves. He demonstrates its deadly weight
when Helen accidentally drops it to the floor, making a loud
sound. And he dispels curiosity and comment about its unusually
large size by having Brookfield mechanically and continually
play with it during a scene shortly before Clay's lethal use of
it as a club.

Settings and properties often are symbolic in *The Witching
Hour.* The colonial furniture of Jack's combination library and
card room suggests in its simplicity, lack of ostentation, and
solidity Jack's unpretentious but dominant manner. The books,

paintings, and sculptures represent his "intellectual improvement and growth in culture" since opening his gambling establishment, as well as "years of arrested development . . . or retrogression" in spiritual growth.[8] The Minerva bust also represents the calmness of wisdom, though beset by doubt in its quest to understand the ultimate nature of reality, which is represented by the Sphinx. The "inert touch of the lower lip against the uncovered teeth" of the Napoleon death mask symbolizes the role of fate, and the marine picture, the existence of an infinite mind at the base of reality. The bust of the religious mystic Dante and the mask of Beethoven, "the mystic of melody," symbolize those men who look behind the material world in their attempt to understand ultimate reality.[9]

The Witching Hour is a broad statement of Thomas's psychic hypotheses. It develops his concepts of the psychic-moral relationship, telepathy, hypnosis, suggestion, and "meaningful coincidence" and suggests his belief in the basically psychic nature of the universe—the existence of an infinite subjective mind, possessing the traits of finite subjective minds and evolutionally expressing itself through natural laws on the stage of history and the material world.

The Harvest Moon (1909). Since *The Witching Hour* was the most successful play in America in 1907, it is not surprising that Thomas continued in the psychic vein with *The Harvest Moon.* In his background reading for *The Witching Hour,* he had collected, he thought, a "fund of information that would have served for fifty plays."[10] Believing that the public was now interested in subtle psychological theses, Thomas based *The Harvest Moon* on modern psychological findings about the law of suggestion, the kinship of color and emotion, and personality disorders. His authoritative spokesman in the play for recent psychological theories is Monsieur Vavin. Though a French playwright by profession, he is a friend of the famous neurologist Charcot and with him has engaged in psychic experiments. He understands well recently discovered psychological laws, psychological types, and characterization according to instinct dominance. In function, he is the heroine's psychotherapist, and the play is an adaptation in dramatic form of her psychotherapeutic case, diagnosis, and cure. Dora Fullerton, raised as the daughter of Harvard University Professor Fullerton, is repeatedly told

by Fullerton and his sister, Cornelia, that she has inherited her
dead mother's vacillation and waywardness. Consequently, she
runs away from school, accepts and then breaks an engagement
with Graham Winthrop, and determines against the Fullertons'
wishes to become an actress. Vavin, who had taught Dora while
she was in France, is called to the professor's home in act 1
to counsel her against acting; but finding her motivation sound,
he recommends the theater for her.

By the second act, set at the Winthrop's New York home
between the dress rehearsal and Dora's opening performance,
Winthrop, the author of the play, has labeled her love scenes
with the leading man as "vulgar," and a lover's quarrel has
ensued. When Dora refuses to act on opening night, Vavin
discerns that Dora's momentary interest in the leading man was
due to negative suggestion by the theatrical company that she
would succumb to the actor whom no woman can resist.
Through suggestions, Vavin convinces a family friend, Judge
Elliott, and then the family that the judge is ill, thus demonstrating the effect of eighteen years of suggestion on an impressionable girl. Dora is persuaded to act.

By the third act, the play has been unsuccessful. Vavin, in
his apartment, prompts the still estranged Winthrop and Dora
to rehearse the love scene in the play with a different lighting
and while moonlight flows through the apartment's window.
He steps outside, and the rehearsal becomes a reconciliation
of the author and actress. In act 4 Dora learns that Fullerton
is not her real father, and that her mother, driven to France
by the Fullertons' suggestion that she had a wicked temperament, had divorced Fullerton before giving birth to her daughter. Dora's plans to leave the Fullertons' home immediately
and not to marry Winthrop are prevented when Vavin reveals
she is his daughter and that a quarrel had led her mother
to leave Vavin and without his knowledge give birth to a
child.

The themes in the play are the effect of suggestion on character
formation, the responsibility in turn of each person for his suggestions, and the effect of color on emotions. During the play,
negative suggestions are made by Cornelia to Dora and by Vavin
to Judge Elliott and, before the time of the play, by Fullerton
and Vavin to Beatrice. Positive suggestion is made by Vavin

and Holcomb to Dora. The individual's responsibility for his suggestions, implied by the effect of suggestion on character development, is further elaborated through Vavin's view of each playwright's responsibility for the suggestions in his play. The effect of color on emotions is demonstrated when Vavin changes the lighting of the play-within-the-play during Holcomb and Dora's private rehearsal.

During the play, Cornelia constantly insinuates that Beatrice was "wayward and unreliable, impulsive and perverse" and suggests that Dora has inherited similar tendencies toward "wilfulness," "slyness," "ungratefulness," "vanity and vicious perverseness," "foolish talk about expression—wanting to live her life," and desire to join the theater.[11]

Dora's actions and decisions often do seem ill considered and inconsistent: she runs away from school; accepts, but then discontinues, her engagement to Graham; vulgarly performs a love scene with the leading man Ludlow, but becomes enraged when criticized for her manner of acting; and overrides her family's opposition to a stage career, only to refuse to perform on opening night. Her motivation often seems self-centered: she appears to jilt Graham; in refusing to act on opening night, she seems not to consider the preparation and livelihood of others involved in the performance of the play; and she rejects the sincere offers of hospitality of Mrs. Winthrop, generosity by Fullerton, and marriage by Holcomb.

By nature, however, Dora has very desirable qualities: an artistic sensibility and potentiality, an expressive personality, and an altruistic moral nature. Her artistic sensibility is revealed through her need of expression; her potentiality, through her appearance, carriage, and charisma. Her expressive personality is evidenced by her extroversion and strong ego; and her moral nature, by her altruistic motivation throughout the play, even for actions apparent to others as self-motivated. Her anger at Holcomb and subsequent refusal to accept the Winthrops' hospitality, for example, are based on altruistic impulses. Her anger at Holcomb is intractable because it is directed primarily at herself for immorally becoming fascinated with the lead man in the play. She will not stay at the Winthrops' because she will not trade on Mrs. Winthrop's desire to see Dora and Graham married. Likewise, she will not accept Fullerton's offer of a home at the end of the play because she is not legally his daughter; nor will she marry Holcomb, because he deserves a wife with estimable parentage and may someday regret her illegitimacy.

Thus, Dora possesses very positive character traits, but often demonstrates irrational behavior. Its etiology is not bad genes transmitted from mother to daughter, but Cornelia's, as well as Fullerton's, misinterpretation of character (both Beatrice's and Dora's) because of a distorting Puritan perspective, misapplication of a faulty theory of heredity, and dispensation of negative suggestions. Fear that Dora will inherit Beatrice's "instability, vacillation, impulsiveness, vanity" (actually a misinterpretation of Beatrice's perseverance and courage) leads Cornelia, with good intentions, to forewarn Dora about a possible similar deviation. This prognosis, however, creates in Dora's mind fears that lead to self-doubt, and self-doubt can lead to failure through lack of confidence rather than lack of ability. Negative suggestion tends to produce the consequence it aims to prevent, as in the example of the young man imprisoned for forgery, not because he is naturally criminal, but because as a boy he was frequently reminded that his uncle had been incarcerated for the same crime.

To isolate negative suggestion as the only cause of Dora's abnormal behavior, Thomas gives her an ideal parentage, a "gentle mother of cultivated stock and fine training, and . . . a father of intellectual power and notable achievement," and has her raised in "wholesome and sustaining surroundings," a "safe New England household where all the inducements are to a well-ordered life" (4–5). Dora's joining the stage and her fascination with Ludlow are partly the fruit of negative suggestion. She repeatedly has been told that she inherits a propensity for stage life and that this life is improper for a young girl. Mrs. Winthrop calls a theatrical career a "lifelong blight" (19); Graham claims she is "too good" for it, and the Judge feels it lowers her standards (47–48). Dora, because of Cornelia's low estimate of her character and theory of heredity, partly resigns her responsibility to decide whether she should join the stage. The members of the theatrical company, believing that Dora, like the ingenue in every theatrical company, will become infatuated with Ludlow, offer a positive suggestion that Dora, being

in love with Holcomb, accepts as a negative suggestion. Her
subsequent attraction to Ludlow is only natural.

At a psychologically crucial moment in the play, Vavin demonstrates the effect of negative suggestion on Dora by the "Russian
experiment of telling a well man he is ill" (67). Finding Judge
Elliott's face pale and his eyes unusual in appearance, Vavin
regrets burdening him when he is not well. Further claiming
that the calm judge is excited when he should be resting and
quiet, Vavin questions whether he has pain and feels strong.
Graham begins to notice that Elliott's color "isn't as high as
sometimes," and Mrs. Winthrop, becoming anxious about the
lines of his face, orders him not to stand and suggests a medicinal
tea. The quite healthy judge, who yesterday walked all the way
through Central Park, by now "wouldn't be foolish enough
to try it" (65–66).

Dora's conduct and thought are due to the force of negative
suggestion on her natural character. She possesses the qualities
of independence and need of self-expression that she inherited
from her mother; from her environment she has "inherited"
an image of herself as impulsive and doomed to moral failure.
Her natural and acquired impulses combat one another during
the play. All her seeming vacillation is due to this struggle;
all the periods of stability in consistent behavior and thought
stem from the dominance of one of these forces and the repression or latency of the other.

Dora's self-reliance, for example, as well as the unpleasantness
of Cornelia, leads her to run away from school, but Cornelia
convinces her she is growing up like her mother and that "a
girl who ran away from her school couldn't hope for much"
(49). So Dora hastily accepts the proposal of the first person
to console her and thus assure her of self-worth. Naturally, in
a less self-incriminating mood, her strength of character prompts
her to break the engagement. The same independence of spirit
and firmness of character motivate her persistence in pursuing
a theatrical career, but self-doubts cause her to refuse temporarily to perform on the opening night of Holcomb's play. Agreeing
with Holcomb's charge that her love scene with Ludlow was
vulgarly acted, she feels that she is shallow, that she cannot
trust herself in her relationship with the leading man, and that
she is not good enough for Holcomb. The same self-doubt lies

behind her avoidance of Holcomb during the first few performances of the play. Cornelia's later revelation that Dora's father
was a "scamp" only makes Dora more critical of her own worth.
She feels that the servant Mrs. Blair is better than she, that
she does not deserve a future, and that she should have a hard-
working and poor-paying job.

Dora, of course, is as susceptible to positive suggestion as
to negative. Holcomb's confidence in her acting ability enables
her to speak the lines of the ill Miss Metcalfe. Vavin, however,
is mainly responsible for replacing the negative suggestions in
Dora's mind with curative and positive ones. Thus he convinces
Dora to act on the opening night of the play by arousing her
pride in her beauty and in the "beautiful moment" of a personal
triumph, and her concern for Holcomb and his future. To focus
Dora's attention on her beauty during his hypnotic suasion,
Vavin holds a mirror in front of her face; this technique also
allows Dora to see her facial reactions to the sentiments he is
conveying. Thus she is able to see what she feels.

Vavin also uses suggestion to bring Holcomb and Dora back
together after their initial estrangement. Having invited them
to his hotel rooms, he relaxes them by serving oyster crabs
Newburgh and wine and then has them perform a flirtatious
love scene in the play so he can make directorial suggestions
and show the effect of lighting. Their acting of a love scene
naturally brings their restrained feelings for each other to the
surface. Vavin repeatedly tells them to smile, knowing that actions suggest emotions. The man who smiles, even in acting,
soon feels like smiling.

Holcomb had employed the depressing color of brown or a
dark blue for the apartment walls, but Vavin substitutes red
lighting for this "cooing physical love" scene (86), and Dora
and Holcomb feel the different atmosphere that the variation
in lighting creates. In his experiments with Charcot, Vavin explains, they discovered the "effect of color upon many persons
under hypnotic influences. . . . Invariably under yellow the
subject laughs; under green he is content; under red he is content
also, but slightly stimulated; if it is brown he is in fear; if violet
he weeps; under blue there is a—what do you call it manner—
distrait?" (80–81).

For another scene in Holcomb's play with the sentiments of

night but played in white light, Vavin suggests the theatrical
use of moonlight, which combines the "blue light, which is
mystery; and the green light, which is content" (87), as appropriate for this love scene "of adoration . . . where the woman is
on a pedestal" (86). He then explains that the harvest moon
appears at almost the same time for three nights instead of an
hour later each night so that the harvesters will fall in love.
Vavin opens the curtains of the window, and the scene is played
in moonlight, while he leaves to answer a nonexistent telephone
call. By now, the food, wine, acting out of love scenes, and
moonlight have expressed their suggestions. When Vavin returns, Dora is exclaiming "I do—I do" to Holcomb's request
that she say she loves him.

Lighting is used not only to affect the emotions of Dora and
Holcomb, but also to create through suggestion a certain mood
in the audience. Thus, Thomas's theory not only is dramatized
on the stage but is also demonstrated by the reaction of the
audience. The audience response, however, derives as much
from Vavin's vocal suggestion of the effect of the colors as
from their visual impact.

The love scene rehearsal, through suggestion, also serves to
improve Dora's professional ability. Her performance would
be hampered by the stigma she mentally associates with the
scene, the cause of friction with Holcomb. That stigma is now
removed; from now on when she flirts with Ludlow in the play,
she will be flirting mentally with Holcomb. Having more confidence in her character, she will perform better as an actress.

In the last act, Vavin again resorts to positive suggestion when
Dora, having been told she is fatherless, has decided to quit
the stage. He arouses her pride in the "courage of that nose,
that firm jaw" and in her decision to say "I will do my work
in the theatre"; to forestall self-pity, he states that "from suffering
comes pity . . . for someone else who suffers, too" and from
"pity—comes the human love and then help and then altogether
we broken-hearted . . . we wounded ones—we cripples—we
take one step—forward" (102-3). To Dora's belief that she
cannot return to the stage, Vavin replies:

> *Vavin.* Don't hear yourself speak that—say I'll try. (Pause.) With
> me—"I'll try."

Dora.   Yes.

Vavin.   The words, "I'll try."

Dora.   I'll try. (104)

His final suggestion is the revelation that he is her father, a revelation that he had not made earlier, for the strongest suggestion comes from helping yourself: "We are not strong when one *lifts* us from our despair—only when we *ourselves* climb" (107).

The responsibility of the individual for his suggestion, dramatized in Dora's character formation, is also implied both in Beatrice's fate—the consequence of Fullerton's suggestion that "she was frivolous and foolish to sing" and Vavin's suggestion that "she was not a wife—when she was yet a mother" (106)—and in Holcomb's profession. Holcomb is a dramatist because he sees in his mind "men and women collide" and wants his actors to imitate what he sees. The public is moved "to *think*—to say—to do—the same things" performed by the actors, especially since no man's suggestion "is so subtle—so sure—so strong—as the suggestion the playwright makes from the stage to the people" and since suggestion is most readily accepted in a crowd (75). Thus through his plays the dramatist has the duty to help the public "look up" (107).

In *The Harvest Moon,* as in *The Witching Hour,* Thomas appealed to the instincts and personified the forces in the play. The most salient technique based on psychic theories, however, is Thomas's suggestive use of setting. Besides the color variation in act 3, Thomas chose the color, furniture, and other equipment of each act "with a view of heightening the effect of the idea expressed" in that particular section of the play. For example, the "considerable elevation" of Vavin's room, its pale gray wall and matching carpet, white side lights over the mantel, lighted and trimmed fire, and "style and trimming of the furniture" contribute to the impression of a "secure" grasp of life and "profound" feeling. In contrast, the gold and green Louis XV furniture, hangings, and rug; bibelot; pedestals; and statuettes in Mrs. Winthrop's drawing room suggest a "light and insincere" mental attitude and "superficial view of life." The harsh angularity, lead color, and heavy furniture of Fullerton's studio symbolize, however, the oppressive puritanical environment in which Dora is raised.[12]

As a Man Thinks (1911). *The Harvest Moon* had an anemic run of some sixteen weeks, but *As a Man Thinks,* Thomas's best play, was one of the biggest hits of 1911. Thomas described Samuel Seelig, his representative of the great American Jew, as "philanthropic, far seeing [an etymological pun on *telepathy*] and, above all, sweetly domestic."[13] Seelig, a millionaire Jewish physician in New York City, performs many charities, including free clinical surgery. He is a modern Christ figure (partially the embodiment of Thomas's desire to write a modern passion play) and spokesman, through both words and deeds, for several of Thomas's basic philosophies: the need for a belief in one Being greater than humans, altruism in emotions and actions, calm acceptance of the higher responsibilities of life, and serenity.

During the play, Elinor Clayton deduces a past infidelity by her husband and defiantly accompanies Benjamin De Lota, a Jewish writer and art critic and one of her former suitors, to his hotel. When Frank Clayton, her husband and a successful publisher of several metropolitan newspapers and periodicals, learns of this event, he orders her to leave his home, but Dr. Seelig tells Clayton that their eight-year-old son, Dick, is critically ill. Clayton takes residence at his club and later, doubting the legitimacy of his son, becomes psychosomatically ill. In act 3, Elinor, temporarily staying at the Seeligs', simmers with resentment over the sexual double standard in this *"man's world."* Seelig administers to her mind, explaining that in a nonsocialist state, in which the family is the unit of social structure, a woman has less sexual liberty than a man because she has a greater responsibility. A woman knows or may know her children's father, but a father's sureness of his paternal relationship depends on his faith in the woman. Instead of resenting discrimination and being jealous, Mr. and Mrs. Clayton and De Lota, who is discriminated against racially, should forgive and sweetly bear their crosses, as Seelig must do in the last act, when he learns his daughter has married a non-Jewish sculptor. In act 4, Seelig ministers to Clayton and engineers a reconciliation between the husband and wife.

The central theme of *As a Man Thinks* is the toxic and tonic properties of emotions: selfish emotions, such as anger, resentment, and anxiety, generating poisons in the body, and altruistic emotions producing physical well being. Other primary themes

include the oneness of all being and the need for a double
standard of morality for the sexes and for the forgiveness of
sin.

Dr. Seelig, though Thomas's advocate for mental healing in
the play, is not a Christian Scientist who believes that all disease
is mentally produced. In act 4, for instance, Seelig first diagnoses
Clayton's illness for physical etiology before positing psychological causes. Then he explains to him the physiological side of
emotions. Clayton's grouch, for example, constantly generates
a medically incurable internal poison. Hate kills the hater; it
conceives one of the deadliest poisons in nature. Seelig further
tutors Clayton, explaining that Christ expressed the psychologi-
cal-physiological correlation, which is the "essence" of "Life,"
in his phrase "As a man thinketh."[14] Christ's *"Forgive,* and ye
shall be forgiven; *give* and it shall be given unto you" is a "good
working rule of life," for good will, not interchangeable with
peace is "active . . . a constructive force." Because of an "influence circulating through all men when they'll permit it, just
as the current through that lamp goes through all other lamps
in this house," sick people have gotten well "merely through
two or three hearty good wishers rooting for them." Stop the
current, however, "by avarice or cupidity, divert it by envy,
turn it back by hate, and something goes wrong with the machinery" (197).

Thomas illustrates this physiological property of emotions
through Elinor's insomnia in act 1, Frank's illness in act 4, and
Dick's illness in acts 2, 3, and 4. Elinor's inability to sleep is
due not to a physiological dysfunction but to her inability to
forgive Frank's "mistake" in Atlantic City and her anxiety about
its recurrence. Similarly, in act 4, Frank's pain and "rotten"
feeling (190), suggested by his dress of gown and slippers and
his reclining on a couch under a steamer rug, stem from his
bitter suspicions about Elinor and De Lota and his hatred of
De Lota; the wrinkle between his eyes grows from the "wrin-
kles" in his mind (193–94).

Frank and Elinor's unhealthy emotions impair not only themselves but also Dick, who has none of Elinor's resentment of
the double standard or Frank's jealousy. Unaware of the family
friction, he knows late in the play only that he is living in a
home not his own and that he has not seen his father for some

time. His fever and irritated throat arise from his subconscious receptivity of the tension in the family, especially in the mind of Elinor. As Seelig notes, "The connection between mother and child is more subtle, more enduring than our physiologies even suggest" (93). The relationship of mother and child in this instance is unusually intimate, for Elinor, often separated from Frank because of his work and her fears, becomes emotionally dependent on Dick. This dependence, naturally mutual, creates a sensitive rapport between the two and even results in telepathy. Once, with Dick asleep, Elinor is reading one of Frank Stockton's stories about "men carrying sacks of gold from cave to ship," when the child wakes up saying "Where—where's all that money . . . that gold—those men had!" (92–93).

The rapport has also stunted Dick's growth. Elinor's hysteria and her feeling of being neglected have led the child to develop a weak constitution and to lack a healthily aggressive and self-dependent personality. Being insecure, he feels the need for attention and assurance, calling for mama when Elinor leaves to go to the opera and wanting to be carried to the nursery by father when Seelig arrives.

Although Thomas does not develop their physiological symptomatology, he presents three views just as destructive as Elinor's and Frank's anger: prejudice against the Jews, De Lota's resentment of racial discrimination, and Elinor's resentment of the double standard. Frank Clayton and Judge Hoover, Elinor's father, manifest racial bias. Frank hates "cheap" Jews, but admires a "classy Jew with education and culture" who thinks "in compound fractions," while the white Anglo-Saxon Protestant thinks in "vulgar integers." Hoover, however, distrusts the "whole breed," blackballs Seelig's admission to a club, and, without evidence, attributes the libel suit in the play to the Jew De Lota (91, 97–98).

De Lota's resentment of the "price of being a Jew . . . in money—in opportunity—in sensibilities" (161) is as condemnable as Frank's and Hoover's racial bias. This resentment is justly criticized by Seelig, not simply because it influences De Lota's adultery in France and his advances toward Elinor, but also because it violates the Jew's duty to accept suffering. The Jewish historical and ethnic obligation to transmit the belief in one God will result in misunderstanding and mistreatment.

Instead of being cursed by this responsibility, the Jew is blessed. Suffering leads to pity, pity to help, and help to self-help. De Lota should accept his racial burden and help others, as Seelig does, instead of pitying himself.

Women, because of their sex, also have an imposing burden and responsibility:

> Men work for their children because they believe the children are— their own—*believe*. Every mother *knows* she is the mother of her son or daughter. Let her be however wicked, no power on earth can shake that knowledge. Every father believes he is a father only by his faith in the woman. Let him be however virtuous, no power on earth can strengthen in him a conviction greater than that of faith. There is a double standard of responsibility because upon the golden basis of woman's virtue rests the welfare of the world. (147–48).

Elinor's rejection of the double standard and her view of it as a "license for transgression" (78) is destructive to the fabric of society. Women, like Jews, should accept without venom the discrimination against them.

Implied in Thomas's view concerning the double standard is the biological unit of the family as a paradigm of two psychic variables essential to cosmic evolution: the need of expression and ideals. The expressive character, usually localized by Thomas in the male variable—though Dora in *The Harvest Moon* is an exception—clashes, Darwinian fashion, with the environment, thus creating plays, newspapers, bridges. Traveling through experience, the expressive character also encounters temptations, often succumbs to them, and thus learns of the frailty of human nature and the need of forgiving others. Suffering leads to empathy and then to active sympathy.

Women and Jews in the play represent the psychic variable of ideals. Both are discriminated against—women by the double standard, Jews by racial bias. Both possess higher responsibilities: women bear the cross of the sanctity of the home, Jews, the cross of monotheism. Women must not request the same sexual privileges granted by society to men, for at the base of all civilization is the reproductive instinct, involving certainty about the parentage of children. Women and Jews, experiencing discrimination, but forgiving and not discriminating against others, develop respectively those instincts of love of family and love of humanity. They become more altruistic and progress further toward the evolutionary goal of universal altruism. Through their model behavior, they also serve as ideals, those fixed stars by which expressive characters chart their direction.

The therapy prescribed in the play for jaundiced views of life, such as discrimination or resentment of discrimination or psychosomatic diseases, consists of replacing the destructive emotion or viewpoint with a healthy one. Some of the techniques of mental therapy are presented in Elinor's invalid call on Seelig in the first act and Seelig's visit with the ill Frank in the fourth act. With Elinor, Seelig uses the technique of positive suggestion to divert her mind from her conception of her present condition and the technique of reexamination of the psychological wound and cultivation of a positive outlook toward the hurt. For Elinor's insomnia the doctor prescribes a point of view: "I don't know a woman in better physical condition" (16). Then he tells her that she has already taken the medicine: "I saw the care go out of those eyes—and the peace come into them." Through this positive suggestion, Elinor believes she is better and *"grate-fully and impulsively takes"* the doctor's hand (20).

The technique of reexamination of illness-provoking traumas is explained by Seelig in surgical terms. A wound that has healed too quickly and only on the surface may have to be surgically reopened. By analogy, mental troubles are best talked about. The purposes of the reexamination are (1) to relieve anxiety, to get the person to assume that the past is past (19–20), and (2) to persuade the person to cultivate a more positive view of the trauma-producing situation. Seelig accomplishes the latter by first attacking Elinor's defenses—her pitying herself ("the hurt was deeper than I knew" [18]) and her rationalization for not forgiving Frank ("it was a good deal for a woman to overlook" [17]). Then he builds up her pride in Frank's importance as a shaper of public opinion and her role in his success: "Your abiding love for him made all the difference between success and failure. All the forces radiating from Frank really do so because of your loyalty at a supreme moment" (19).

Seelig's visit to Frank in act 4 also begins with his attempt to divert Frank's mind from his present conception of his state of health. He opens the window to let fresh air in and to let

Frank hear the ringing of Christmas bells. He hopes the merriment usually associated with Christmas will stimulate a change in Frank's attitude. Thus he mentions the "wonderful sight on the avenue" of the prosperous Christmas shoppers. Trying to cause Frank to think of others instead of himself, he tells of an "accident to a little chap on Third Avenue—they brought him to the hospital—smaller than your boy" (191). When this approach fails, he tries to divert Frank's mind by getting him to relax, first his hand and then his whole body.

When diversionary tactics fail to change Frank's mood, Seelig prods him into reexamining from a different perspective than before the grounds of his hatred and thoughts of murder. Through his neglect, Frank is partly responsible for De Lota's attention to Elinor. De Lota only "did what nine men out of ten would do" and would "walk around the Belt Line to-night in the snow, barefooted, to have the record closed." Hatred is toxic and often is determined mainly by public opinion of appropriate responses for certain situations (196). Besides, satisfied revenge is disappointing. Frank should look forward instead of backward, for if the doctor can get a patient to realize "that yesterday is yesterday, that his past life doesn't concern him anymore than last year's snow" and get him "looking ahead—hopeful—anxious to get on the job—why he's cured." To Frank's attitude that it is too late to forget the past, the doctor replies by using the parable of the eleventh hour, in which "those who had worked one hour got as much as those who had put in a full day": "You get that peace of mind, whenever—you work, whenever you *do* something—and the splendid thing is, it's *never too late to do it*" (198–99). At this juncture, Seelig, reinforcing his exposition by position and movement, vigorously rises.

Seelig is advocating in the last quotation another technique of mental therapy, based on Thomas's view of the cultivation of the will as "merely a question of mental attitude . . . one of decision—attack—one of impact."[15] One should act in a manner that suggests a positive emotion as motivation for one's action. If one wants to overcome his hatred of another, he should do something that would be symptomatic of a positive, or at least a neutral, emotion; for example, Frank can allow De Lota to leave his magazine without writing a negative reference. If

Frank wants to rebuild the marriage with Elinor, then he should put himself in a situation that suggests that the marriage has been reconstructed, for example, sharing Christmas with Elinor and Dick. If the desired situations are too formidable to act out, then one should start with simpler action, which Seelig calls the "work that's nearest to you": "If I wanted you to walk around Central Park you would have to get up; you would have to walk to the door; you would have to go down the steps; you would have to *walk* to Central Park. In other words, you would have to cover the ground that is nearest to you" (200). If Frank wants to feel well, he should open the windows and let fresh air in, pick up his clothes, and straighten the pictures in his lounging room. These actions would evoke the positive suggestion that he is well. At least he can take a ride in the car, which would place him in an environment without negative associations.

Especially in his altruism and inner peace, Seelig is an avatar of, as well as spokesman for, Thomas's psychic viewpoints about positive character development. He has attained what James Allen in *As a Man Thinketh* called the state of serenity, a calmness of mind dependent upon self-control and an understanding of the "laws and operations of thought." Allen's book, which Thomas owned, is responsible for the title of the play and probably for many of the viewpoints in it. The serene man, according to Allen, realizes that character, circumstances in life, and health are rooted in thought; for example:

Sickly thoughts will express themselves through a sickly body. Thoughts of fear have been known to kill a man as speedily as a bullet, and they are continuously killing thousands of people just as surely though less rapidly. The people who live in fear of disease are the people who get it. Anxiety quickly demoralises the whole body, and lays it open to the entrance of disease, while impure thoughts, even if not physically indulged, will soon shatter the nervous system.

Strong, pure, and happy thoughts build up the body in vigour and grace. (35–36)

The serene man is also successful and is loved, respected, and trusted by others: others "reverence his spiritual strength, and feel they can learn of him and rely upon him" (60).

Seelig manifests the qualities of Allen's serene man. He repeatedly prescribes the cultivation of calmness and demonstrates his possession of it when he learns his car has been borrowed without his permission, that he cannot go to the opera, and that his daughter has married against his wishes. He is successful, respected by others, and espouses the relationship between thought and health.

Many details in the play are influenced by Thomas's psychic theories. Instincts are appealed to; forces are personified; the libretto and two sculptures by Burrill in Seelig's lounging room are repetitive props; Christmas, as well as Seelig's profession, is symbolic of the themes; and the bells of Christmas are aurally suggestive. The settings in the play are also significant. For example, the illustrations in Clayton's lounging room in act 2 suggest his profession, the "square and shallow low" structure of the room, his state of mind, and the green canvas covering the walls, his jealousy. The red hallway at the back of the room probably suggests his anger. The same lounging room in act 4, with its pictures awry and "look of general desolation," symbolizes Frank's mood and state of being at the time. The heavy, solid furniture, picture frames, and beams in the ceiling in Seelig's library suggest his solidity of character, and the picture of Judith over the mantel, his religious orientation.

Minor Plays

Though Thomas's name became indelibly associated with the psychic play only with the production of *The Witching Hour, The Harvest Moon,* and *As a Man Thinks,* he refers to and dramatizes psychological and psychic subjects in a number of other plays. The only incidental appearance of these subjects before the production of *The Witching Hour* reveals how much A. M. Palmer's refusal to produce *A Constitutional Point* and the failures of *New Blood* and *The Capitol* delayed Thomas's staging of serious supernormal and pathological subjects. *A Leaf from the Woods,* one of his earliest plays, includes mention of intuition, the magnetic influence a woman can exert on men—both of which later are more explicitly labeled as psychic phenomena—and a sketch of a psychic personality in Dan Harris, the prototype of Jack Brookfield in *The Witching Hour.* Like Brookfield, Harris is a gambler, and his extraordinarily good luck at cards, as well as his charisma, are attributable to his psychic powers. *Reckless Temple* (1890) presents a fuller dramatization of a psychic personality in the lawyer Temple. Temple has a hypnotic gaze, gives an inspired defense of an accused murderer by using images to arouse emotions, and is, like Harris, charismatic. Telepathy, dramatized in *The Witching Hour,* is earlier alluded to in *Afterthoughts* (1891)—as "mental telegraphy," Thomas's first explicit reference to psychic phenomena—and in *Colonel Carter of Cartersville* (1892), *Champagne Charlie* (1901), and *DeLancey* (1905). Before *The Witching Hour,* hypnotism is slenderly treated in *Alabama* (1891) and *The Meddler* (1898). And coincidence is attributed to statistical probability in *A Man of the World* (1883), fate in the one-act *A Proper Impropriety* (1893) and *De-Lancey,* and unknown psychological or physical laws in *Mrs. Leffingwell's Boots* (1905). Before *The Harvest Moon,* Thomas dramatizes two pathological cases. In *Reckless Temple,* a locomotive engineer is a victim of compulsive behavior because of a persistent guilt complex about his sister's death and the derangement of her illegitimate child.

The Jucklins (Philadelphia, 1897), a melodrama with the local color of a North Carolina backwoods community, is an advanced psychological study of the effect of repressed awareness on behavior. The plot primarily revolves around the love relationship of Alf Jucklin and Millie Lundsford and the apparent insanity of Limuel Jucklin, Alf's father. The so-called insanity resulted from a physical blow received by Limuel when his best friend, Carroll Lundsford, unfairly won a fight by swinging a stone against Limuel's head. The fracas causes Limuel no conscious conflict, but creates a subconscious trauma that dominates his character in stressful situations. Limuel, whose mind under normal circumstances is always reliable and who possesses the ability to be a governor, becomes under great strain abnormally preoccupied with his fighting cocks.

As a result of the psychic trauma caused by the trial of Alf for the murder of a rival for Millie, Limuel temporarily frees himself from his fixation on the fighting cocks. During the trial, he projects his repressed sense of Lundsford's tacit perjury in not owning up to the unfairness of their fight onto Doctor Etheridge's testimony that he had done an autopsy on Alf's rival, and intuits the doctor's lie. Limuel's awareness of the doctor's conscious concealment of the truth also serves as a transferred, symbolic, yet healing awareness of his own subconscious concealment of the fight tactics used by Lundsford.

Three of Thomas's plays after the production of *The Harvest Moon* provide developed but, from an aesthetic and historical perspective, insignificant treatments of psychic or psychological phenomena. In *The Matinee Idol* (1909), adapted from William Bayle Bernard's *His Last Legs,* a play in the Dickson Sketch Club's repertoire, an improvident actor pretending to be a hypnotist doctor at a ladies' seminary seems to cure by hypnosis, induce trances by the passing of hands, and, Svengali-like, teach others to sing through psychic influence. *The Soul Machine* (1915), a melodrama intended for film, stages a life-and-death struggle by psychic villian Doctor Ramsey Gordon Keith to gain mind control over Marion Fenton, who is psychically gifted and thus also psychically susceptible to the villain's hypnotic influence. Doctor Fuller, Marion's uncle, uses psychometry to expose Keith's involvement in several murders. Immediately afterward, Keith swallows a poison and dies, freeing Marion from his hypnotic influence.

Nemesis (1921) includes a Freudian psychoanalyst, a psychological theme—the need of confession—and a number of psychological and psychoanalytic symptoms. A gambling mania is dramatized; social reform is diagnosed as compensation for personal shortcomings, nervous disorders and stammering as indications of hidden guilt, and artistic talent as possible reaction to strict family upbringing. The themes of the play converge in the character of Kallan, whose wife is having an affair with the sculptor Jovaine. Imprinting a rubber stamp with Jovaine's fingertip impressions in studio clay and then transferring the impression to a rubber glove, Kallan places the sculptor's fingerprints on the nail file with which he had killed his wife. Later, outside Sing Sing prison, as a doorway light bulb dims, then brightens, signaling Jovaine's electrocution, Kallan feels compelled to tell the prosecutor that fingerprints can be duplicated.

After burning an incriminating glove finger, he partially confesses to the crime.

A Psychic Era in American Drama

The box-office success of *The Witching Hour* and, to a lesser degree, *As a Man Thinks* convinced theater managers that psychic plays could be profitable ventures. Partially as a result, between 1907 and 1915 a number of American plays staged psychic or psychological material. For example, Charles Klein's *The Third Degree* (1901) and Edwin Milton Royle's *The Unwritten Law* (1913) dramatize hypnotism in relation to the legal system. Psychic vampirism through a combination of mesmerism and telepathy is presented in Edward Allan Woolf and George Sylvester Viereck's *The Vampire* (1909), and traveling clairvoyance in Beulah Marie Dix and Evelyn Greenleaf Sutherland's comedy *The Road to Yesterday* (1907). The influence of mental suggestion on physiological functioning or health appears in Edward Locke's *The Climax* (1909), Frances Hodgson Burnett's *The Dawn of Tomorrow* (1908), and Maurice V. Samuels's *The Conflict* (1909). William Vaughn Moody's *The Faith Healer* (1909) and George M. Cohan's *The Miracle Man* (1914) focus on faith healers, whereas Francis Wilson's *The Spiritualist* (1913) concerns spiritualism and a seance, in which music, strange voices, flashing varicolored lights, and moving furniture are manifest.

Many of the psychic plays were comedies or melodramas, but two, David Belasco's *The Return of Peter Grimm* and Edward Locke's *The Case of Becky,* like Thomas's three major psychic plays, were based on a close reading of contemporary psychic authorities. *The Return of Peter Grimm* (1911) evolved out of Belasco's lifelong interest in the psychic and the supernatural. In the play, Peter Grimm, a Dutch florist, initially represents a skeptical viewpoint toward spirits of the dead existing among the living and influencing their conduct; he dies, but returns ten days later as a spirit to prevent an unwise marriage by his niece. Edward Locke's play on dual personality, *The Case of Becky* (1912), primarily based on Morton Prince's *The Dissocia-*

tion of Personality (1906), was intended as a realistic depiction of the psychotherapy of the first decade of the 1900s.

The psychical period in American drama, conceived with the birth of Thomas's *The Witching Hour,* was dying in 1912 when *The Case of Becky* was first produced. Two reasons for the demise of the psychic play were the rise, in the development of Freudian psychology, of a far more promising subject matter for the play than psychic phenomena and the psychology of Charcot and Janet, and the tapering off of public interest in psychic phenomena. Freudian psychology, which became popular in America after Freud's delivery of the Clark University Lectures in 1909, provided a theory for the deep probing of character, whereas the psychic play was more suited for plot, rather than character, development. After Arthur Hopkins's *The Fatted Calf* (1912), the first American drama seriously treating Freudian theory, multiple personality and Freudian viewpoints were dramatized in a number of plays. Telepathy, however, was rarely dramatized, and hypnotism appeared primarily as a clinical technique. After 1912, psychic plays never were as popular as they had been during the preceding five years.

Similarly, professional and public interest in psychic phenomena, firmly established in the 1880s and rampant at the turn of the century, noticeably waned after World War I. The rapprochement between psychology and psychical science, possible in the 1910s, did not occur. Psychology, a new discipline, gained wider acceptance by the established scientific community by divesting its association with psychical research. Typical of this trend was Ernest Jones's dissuasion of Freud from reading at the 1922 International Psychoanalytic Congress an essay called "Psychoanalysis and Telepathy." Abnormal psychology, which had been part of psychic investigation, became a field in itself, jettisoning the mystical and fraudulent overtones of psychic material. Psychology was the young giant. Interest was focused on this more experimental discipline, in which, in contrast to the field of psychical research, major advances were to be made during the next two decades.

Though a psychic period in American drama did not revive with the rise of parapsychology after 1933, the turn-of-the-century movement is historically, theatrically, and dramatically important. Psychic plays, in general, mirrored contemporary scientific and pseudoscientific thought and zeitgeist. More important, serious dramatic studies of paranormal events, pathological states, and subconscious-mind processes—initiated by *The Witching Hour, The Harvest Moon,* and *As a Man Thinks,* but continued by *The Return of Peter Grimm* and *The Case of Becky*—contributed to the trend toward American problem plays after 1906 and the maturing of American drama after World War I.

Chapter Seven

An Assessment

A Mirror to America

One of Augustus Thomas's most important contributions to American drama was the regularity and comprehensiveness with which his seventy-odd plays mirrored contemporary American history, themes, settings, and people. Of his thirty-five full-length original plays, only *Oliver Goldsmith* was not American in subject, only *Colonel George of Mount Vernon* treated distant American history, and only *Alabama* and *The Cricket of Palmy Days* re-created American history remembered only by the older members of the audience. Among the major events captured for the stage were the labor strikes of the 1890s, the 1893–94 passage of the Wilson tariff bill, women's demonstrations for the right to vote, the congressional debate on the St. Lawrence Seaway, and the national debate on Prohibition.

From New York's fashionable Fifth Avenue to its Bowery, from Washington's Capitol Hill to Missouri's capital, from poverty-stricken Vincennes, Indiana, to western mining camps, Thomas caught the local flavor of the country's settings and people. Against realistic backdrops of the environment, he depicted local idiosyncrasies and point of view, the period, the station of the people, and their speech and dress. He also portrayed peculiarly American characteristics: freedom of individuality, thorough equalitarianism, and a tendency to idealize.

Studying the interaction of character and environment, Thomas made the setting more than a realistic backdrop. The American setting—as in the languorous South of *Alabama,* the Spartan Pike County of *In Mizzoura,* and the barren alkali desert of *Arizona*—also conditioned character and affected plot development. The influencing environment may be mental instead of physical, such as the effect of suggestion on character in *The*

Witching Hour, The Harvest Moon, and *As a Man Thinks.* The interaction may be emotional and physiological, such as the interplay of health and hatred or jealousy in *As a Man Thinks.* Thomas's plays depicted historical fads—such as bicycling in *The Capitol,* smoking by women in *The Meddler,* and renewed interest in boxing after the repeal of the Horton Law in *The Other Girl*—but, more important, they reflected the national concerns of the time. In capturing the mood of the hour—as in *Alabama, Arizona, The Witching Hour, As a Man Thinks,* and *The Copperhead*—Thomas's plays not only mirrored history; they helped shape it and give it expression. *Alabama* did more to heal the rift between the North and South, said Colonel Henry Watterson, than his twenty years of editorializing in the Louisville *Courier-Journal.*

The care with which Thomas tried to reflect the mood of the American people at a particular historical time can be seen in his thoughts, in September of 1917, on writing a play for an autumn, 1918, New York run. Because the mood of America, if still at war in September of 1918, would be that of England, Thomas decided that A. W. Pinero, James Barrie, or some other Englishman was writing the play he wanted to write and, because of the Englishman's direct experience of the war mood, was writing it better than an American could. After lengthily cataloging likely situations in America if the war had ended or was continuing, Thomas chose to build his play, the unproduced *By-Law No. 5,* from the following conditions, common to both contingencies:

Physically, scarcity of material; high prices; manual application to production; high wages; plain living; heavy taxes. Mental—more diffused information; wider horizons; less provincialism; more democracy; greater freedom between the sexes; an increased respect for women; a greater belief in the heroism of the everyday man; greater moral courage; clearer thinking; more kindness but less "politeness"; more mysticism; more superstition; more ghost stories; a greater love of the ground; youth in the saddle; a greater leaning to Flechner's philosophy; state socialism; mutual helpfulness; increased love of children; increased interest in the Gary school plan.[1]

Thomas's success in mirroring America, her locales, and her people and their tastes is reflected in the headlines to reviews of his regional plays. *Alabama* was characterized, for example, as "An American Play at Last," "A True American Play," and "A Good Thing and Our Own." "Our Drama Looking Up," bannered one headline about the "Full-Blooded American" *In Mizzoura;* "Augustus Thomas Seems to Be the Theatrical Moses, and the Promised Land Is in Sight," claimed another.[2]

Credentials for Portraying America

Proclaiming in 1912 that tomorrow's theater would debate great national questions, Thomas said the "single live wire of common interest" coursing through the nation as a whole was the growing belief that the court system favors moneyed interests.[3] Raised in a nonprovincial midwestern family and always attentive to these live wires of common interest, Thomas was well suited to portray America regionally and nationally. His early association of American districts—their characteristic features, industries, products valuable to the economy, and people—with the politicians he admired made American geography as entertaining to him as a storybook. His observation of America, however, was not bookish. As a *Post-Dispatch* reporter, he covered the first Kansas election in which women voted and traveled to Indian territory to interview the 1884 Republican presidential nominee, James Blaine. As an actor in the Marion Place Dramatic Club, the John Norton and Vokes companies, and the Dickson Sketch Club, he performed in cities spanning the Midwest, southern Canada, and the near and Deep South. And as a railroad and flour mill representative, business agent for actress Julia Marlowe, and advance agent for mind reader Washington Irving Bishop, Thomas learned America from first-hand observation.

His regular formal schooling having ended when he was thirteen, Thomas's self-education prepared him for a profession without curriculum or diploma. Working in various sections of railway freight departments between the ages of thirteen and twenty-two and taking his midday meals with Irish freight handlers on the platforms, brakemen in switch shanties, engineers and firemen in their cabs, or trainmen on the running boards of box cars, Thomas became familiar with the economic conditions of the working class during the depression of the

1870s. Having worn homemade nightgowns of coarse cotton flour sacks during financially lean days and having refused a scholarship to study art in Paris and an appointment to West Point so he could help support his family, Thomas could well sympathize with the hard lives of the workers and their political needs. A son of a politically active family and a political cartoonist for the St. Louis *World,* Thomas was knowledgeable about local, state, and national politics. As a page in the Missouri Legislature, he witnessed the adoption of the Fifteenth Amendment giving blacks the right to vote; as a page in the Forty-first Congress, he watched the long session of Reconstruction. He knew from firsthand experience parliamentary procedures, political strategems, the statesmen of his day, and their debates on the country's major issues.

Influenced by the reporter's respect for accuracy and detail and Emerson's dictum to "look in your heart and write," Thomas believed literature should come straight from the soil, with no middleman. In composing *Alabama,* he relied not only on his observation of the ruined Talladega gateway during the Dickson Sketch Club's second tour and his overall knowledge of the South, its land and people, he also drew on his experience of living in a provost marshall–governed city during the Civil War, his knowledge of provisional government and Reconstruction legislation, his twenty-year familiarity with Alabama's apportionment, and his conversations about Alabama's traditions with Muskogee chieftains. Trips to Bowling Green, Missouri, Fort Grant, Arizona, and the San Carlos Indian outpost, Colorado mines, and Rio Grande military outposts prefaced respectively his regional plays *In Mizzoura, Arizona, Colorado,* and *Rio Grande.* Scenery was usually developed from sketches of the regions drawn during his visits or, in the case of *The Earl of Pawtucket,* during a forty-dollar one-night stay at the Waldorf Astoria. Thomas was equally painstaking when he could not travel to the region or site of his play, as when he corresponded with the Missouri governor's secretary to establish for *The Member from Ozark* details of the Missouri House Mansion.

Because Thomas believed in writing from his own experience, published literature played a small role in influencing his development. The one-act plays of William Dean Howells, to which he was introduced during his impressionable Dickson Sketch

Club days, guided Thomas in the development of crisp dialogue and tight play structure and emphasis on character instead of action. Bret Harte's influence is particularly evident in the rough and good-hearted characters of *In Mizzoura* and *The Cricket of Palmy Days* and the recitation of lines from Harte's "The Newport Legend" in *The Witching Hour*. The philosophy of Ralph Waldo Emerson—its American roots, emphasis on self-reliance, and theories such as compensation and fate—was the single major literary influence on Thomas. The playwright, familiar with Emerson's writings from the early 1880s on, read and reread Emerson's essays and journals. The Concord edition of Emerson's complete works were the first books Thomas purchased for the library of his New Rochelle home.

Seriousness in Purpose and Practice

Thomas not only mirrored his experience of America in his plays; he also took a stand on major issues. In treating reconciliation of the North and South, *Alabama* became a historical, as well as a theatrical, event. *Reckless Temple* criticized social conventions and snobbery; *New Blood,* the formation of trusts; and *The Capitol,* the influence of industry and religion on Congress. *The Capitol* advocated the separation of the powers of church and state; *New Blood* presented a solution to the conflict of capital and labor. *A Member from Ozark* exposed the ways in which a trust attempted to influence legislation. Thomas's psychic-psychological plays developed themes: the dynamic nature of thought and the responsibility of individuals for the quality of their thought in *The Witching Hour,* the effect of suggestion on character and colors on emotions in *The Harvest Moon,* and the body poisons produced by selfish emotions and the physical health produced by altruistic ones in *As a Man Thinks*. *The Model* explored the idealizing function of art; *Indian Summer,* the elevation of mankind through self-sacrifice and the inspiration of women and art. *Nemesis* examined Freudian psychology and a potential injustice from courtroom use of fingerprint evidence; *Still Water* propagandized for the end of Prohibition.

For a theater of escapist entertainment, Thomas, when he wrote from his own experience, wrote purposive plays. Consciously or unconsciously, the playwright, he thought, stirred emotions, strengthening the audience's criminal or heroic tendencies and advancing or retarding the species' evolution toward altruistic civilization. His plays from the soil thus were entertaining but serious business.

As conscientious in craft as in subject matter, Thomas learned his dramatic technique not only from years of apprenticeship in the theater as a writer, actor, and director but also from studiously constructed psychological theories. Over the years he developed the first comprehensive and systematic theory of playwriting by an American dramatist, and he put the theory into practice. The powers, faculties, and characteristics of the subconscious mind, as he understood them, inspired his plot construction, selection of dramatis personae, personification of forces, appeal to instincts, repetitive use of properties, and suggestive and symbolic use of setting and properties.

He also put other workshop insights into practice. He tried to know his characters from the cradle so he could apprehend the hidden springs of character behind their action, such as education, religion, and politics. He clearly established his characters; though he entertained by surprise, he never put his audience on a false scent. Characters and ideas, as well as properties, important later in the play were identified early. Lines were laconic and the vocabulary simple, except for the effect of humor. Overlapping cues between lines were provided by looks and gestures. Each line advanced the story, developed character, or got a laugh. Incidents accelerated as the play progressed, with later scenes having shorter and thicker trajectories than earlier ones because the audience's attention gradually wanes and strong scenes seem to pass more quickly than weak ones. The number of persons and the tonal quality of scenes were varied. The emotional explosion near the fall of the curtain was left as suspense and followed with extrication. And each act was treated separately as a one-act idea.

Besides trying to improve the quality of American drama through the subject matter and craft of his own plays, Thomas also sought to forge a link between the professional and the art theater. As early as January of 1912, he met with A. L. Erlanger, the head of the Theatrical Syndicate, to garner the backing of American managers for a stock theater in which the best classical and modern plays would be performed by the best American actors in the best productions. In December of 1922, as executive chairman of the Producing Managers' Association and spokesman for the organized theater, he urged the establishment of a permanent art theater in New York, which would produce primarily, but not exclusively, Shakespearean plays.

Believing the theater belonged not to the managers, playwrights, or actors but to the public, he called for a national theater. Trying to enlist the involvement of all American managers and even the motion picture industry, he wanted to take Broadway to Kokomo, Saginaw, and other little towns by promoting the filming and nationwide distribution of successful plays during their New York runs. Thinking that repetitive assembly-line work would force industrial workers to turn to either the arts or reform for self-expression, he encouraged the growth of community and little theaters, tried to interest professional managers in amateur productions, and promoted the staging of a passion play, a successor to Oberammergau, in every large city. To further interest in and study of drama nationwide, he called for universities and colleges to offer extension courses in drama and sought the cooperation of George Pierce Baker, to whose Harvard University playwriting course Thomas had spoken on 26 February 1912 about the technical side of drama. To focus attention on his craft, he wrote prefaces to eleven of his published plays, describing the techniques and process of construction of each one. His autobiography, *The Print of My Remembrance* (1922), was also written to give advice to young playwrights.

To establish a permanent art theater, Thomas tried to avoid the mistakes of New York's endowed New Theatre, the committee of which had wanted to enlist Thomas as its director after a period of unsuccessful operation from 1909 through 1911. He decided not to build a theater and not to maintain a company with a repertory but rather to typecast actors and hire a theater for a play's run. Though he generated substantial interest and financial and artistic support for the idea of a national theater, his project died abruptly with the newspapers' unanimous condemnation of its opening production of *As You Like It*, particularly of the performance of Marjorie Rambeau, whom Thomas had typecast as Rosalind.

New Directions in American Drama

In presenting American life realistically and sympathetically, combining thought and entertainment in his plays, and improving the technique of American drama, Thomas was more than a mirror to his age. He was a major force in shaping the transition of American drama from 1891 through 1911.

In 1912 Thomas estimated that not more than 10 percent of dramas in American theaters were imported, whereas earlier in his dramatic career at least 50 percent of the plays produced in America were written in France or Germany or rewritten in England.[4] Thomas's first salaried position as a dramatist was as A. M. Palmer's reviser and adapter of foreign plays. When *Alabama* was first staged, Palmer's audience was accustomed to dull English plays; native playwrights were composing stale farces. When *Arizona* played on the New York stage in September 1900, it competed against the English *Brother Officers* and *The Rose of Persia,* the German *Prince Otto* and *The Husbands of Leonitine,* and the Danish *Ib and Little Christina.*

The popularity of Thomas's *Alabama, In Mizzoura,* and *Arizona,* and his mastery of technique led managers to think that plays about American subjects and by Americans could be financially successful and might even compete with imports in literary quality. *Alabama* and *Arizona* prompted rages for southern and western plays. Charles Frohman commissioned Thomas to write *Surrender* and *Colorado;* A. M. Palmer, who had not produced before *Alabama* a full-length American play since his Union Square Theatre days, asked Thomas to adapt *Colonel Carter of Cartersville.* Though the failure of *New Blood* changed his intentions, Palmer, according to the September 15, 1894, program for the opening of *New Blood,* had planned to follow Thomas's socioeconomic plays with *The Capitol* and a season consisting entirely of American plays at Palmer's Theatre.

Besides widening the stage to include serious plays of the American soil, Thomas assisted in refining the crude melodrama of his time, with its black-and-white heroes and villains, stock characters, sensational plots, and happy endings. Though forced to write theatrical plays when audiences, accustomed to "blood and thunder" melodrama, rejected his realistic plays as drab, Thomas's preference for natural plays written from his own

experience is evident in the quiet humor and pathos and especially in the absence of coarseness in *Editha's Burglar* (1883)
and the absence of firing guns in *The Cricket of Palmy Days*
(1919). Before *Alabama*, Thomas's fidelity to life—"candor"
as he called it—is embodied in the peaceful rural Wisconsin
setting in *A Leaf from the Woods*, Captain Bradley's calm and
judicious defusing of a triangular love relationship in *A Man
of the World*, and the older woman's delicate concealment of
her love for the younger man she persuades to return to his
betrothed in *Afterthoughts*.

Alabama was not withdrawn by Palmer from rehearsals three
times simply because it was American in subject. American characters, settings, and themes had received attention in Bronson
Howard's *The Banker's Daughter* (1878) and *The Henrietta*
(1887), David Lloyd Demarest's *The Senator* (1884), Denman
Thompson's *The Old Homestead* (1887), and Charles Barnard
and Neil Burgess's *The Country Fair* (1889). The South had
been subject matter in Dion Boucicault's *The Octoroon* (1859),
Bartley Campbell's *The Gallery Slave* (Philadelphia, 1879), William Gillette's *Held by the Enemy* (1886), and Howard's *Shenandoah* (1889). Rather, Palmer was reluctant to produce *Alabama*
because of Thomas's untheatrical treatment of an American subject and the unusual breathtaking quietness with which each
act ended. Audiences of Thomas plays, in America and in England, also were surprised by the lack of action and scarcity
of situations and climaxes. Thomas's quiet endings can be seen
particularly in *Alabama, New Blood, The Hoosier Doctor, The Witching Hour, The Harvest Moon, As a Man Thinks, The Model, Indian
Summer, Rio Grande, The Copperhead*, and *The Cricket of Palmy
Days*. This departure from the playwriting practice of never
following a climax with a weaker situation stemmed, in part,
from his newspaper training. A reporter does not stop his article
with a man falling dead in a murder, he said; the reporter follows
the story to the end of its journey, describing the arrival of
the ambulance, the reaction of the sightseers, the effect of the
death on the relatives, and so on. "Why should the curtain
fall at the climax, and then say quarter of an hour later, the
audience be shown what the effect was?"[5]

Except in his more melodramatic plays, like *Arizona* and *Rio
Grande*, Thomas's plots are primarily pegs on which the play-

wright hung studies first of character and setting and later of theme. His characters, overall, were not bookish to his audiences, but like a friend or acquaintance or the girl next door. Character types—such as the squire in *Alabama,* the sheriff in *In Mizzoura,* the Negro servant Chad in *Colonel Carter of Cartersville,* and the physician in *The Hoosier Doctor*—are individualized. In *Alabama,* interest is so diffuse and lavish that the play is practically without a hero and heroine, and the villain is a villain only in his being the worst of the characters. In *Arizona,* character parts are so well subordinated to the overall action that some reviewers identified Denton as the hero; others selected Canby.[6]

In Thomas's plays, conflict is more potential than actual. The multiple plots in his better plays complement each other. The endings, though probably interpreted as happy by Thomas's audiences, are often ambiguous. Does Sheriff Radburn, in *In Mizzoura,* win the hand of Kate Vernon? Is the aging artist in *Indian Summer* joined in Paris by the girl who has learned to perceive beauty through his eyes? Will Colonel Bonham, in *Rio Grande,* reclaim his foolish wife when he returns from Cuba? These and other questions are not directly answered.

Melodrama was redefined by Thomas's practice—not only in form, but also in content. Caspar Harold Nannes separates the advance in political drama into three periods: "before 1900, when the dramatist used political events as window dressing for his plots; from 1900 to 1930, when the playwright attacked specific abuses; and from 1930 to the present, when the author not only attacked abuses but also advocated a philosophy of government for politicians and voters to follow."[7] In 1894 and 1895 respectively, Thomas's *New Blood* and *The Capitol* advocated a philosophy of change in the economic and political systems.

Thomas's theme plays helped clear the way for a serious presentation of ideas on the American stage. Influencing a jury from a distance by one's thought, hypnotizing a man about to pull a revolver trigger, and other such psychic feats were not in Thomas's age "hokum" or "half-baked" ideas, as some have charged. Unlike the sensational melodramas of *Trilby* and *The Bells,* Thomas's *The Witching Hour, The Harvest Moon,* and *As a Man Thinks,* David Belasco's *The Return of Peter Grimm,* Edward Locke's *The Case of Becky,* and the more objective treatment of psychic phenomena in fiction were based on medical research in hypnotism and suggestion, scientific research in psychic phenomena, and contemporary findings in psychology.

Resistance to Change in the American Theater

Thomas's staging of serious thought in plays thoroughly American and his refining of dramatic techniques were evolutions not achieved without a struggle. Until after 1910, when the little theater movement began in America, the American playwright, with few exceptions, had no choice but to write for a highly commercial theater. For a play to be accepted for production, it had to entertain quickly; an unsuccessful play would close within a few days. The audience generally came to see the stable of stars each manager groomed more than the play itself. People came to the theater not to think but to laugh and be moved by the swift action and spectacular scenes of melodrama. Love interest was required, though with unchaperoned women in the audience the exploration of sexual topics was limited: a man and a woman touching hands on stage was serious business.

Until 1910 or so, when the motion pictures began to replace the stage, the play had to appeal to those with university degrees as well as those with less than a high school diploma. It also had to appeal to ethnically diverse audiences, for until 1911 a play had to have promise of success on the road as well as in New York. It could not offend a major segment of the population or be too advanced in thought or experiment, as James Herne learned in his production of *Margaret Fleming* (1890) about marital infidelity. Thomas's *Reckless Temple* failed more because of its criticism of social conventions than its artistic flaws. His *New Blood,* the production of which was delayed for years because of the play's controversial nature, was rejected by New York audiences primarily for the same reason the more proletarian Chicago audiences patronized it—its condemnation of capitalistic practices and upper-class foibles.

The reluctance of theater managers to produce problematic, avant-garde, or controversial plays, even though their subject matter had been popularized in general and in all other literary forms, can be seen in the evolution of *The Witching Hour* from *A Constitutional Point.* Though Thomas had avoided as far as possible spiritism and dealt instead with startling coincidences and seemingly inexplicable intuitions, A. M. Palmer rejected the one-act play in 1890, thinking that audiences would not understand its theme.

Meanwhile, public interest in psychic phenomena increased, finding expression in the growth of organizations such as Christian Science, allegedly supernormal manifestations by individual performers, and scientific and pseudoscientific publications. Besides appearing in magazines and newspapers, psychic phenomena became prevalent in fiction, where they were treated more objectively than earlier in the nineteenth century. This more objective treatment of psychic phenomena was partially a result of medical interest in hypnotism and suggestion by the 1880s and professional interest in psychical investigation by the Society for Psychical Research, founded in 1882, and the American Society for Psychical Research, founded in 1885. Publication of the work of these prestigious psychical societies was not restricted to specialized journals.

By 1905, Thomas felt that interest in psychic phenomena was firmly established, having been developed seriously in all literary forms except the drama, and was almost calling aloud for dramatization. When *The Witching Hour,* primarily composed after a well-received performance of *A Constitutional Point* at the Lambs Club, was presented for production, Daniel Frohman pronounced the author "crazy" to dramatize such a subject; and Charles Frohman advised Thomas to go West and write another wholesome *Arizona.*

Writing for a Commercial Theater

Until about 1907, Thomas and other American playwrights were prisoners of a theatrical organization that made money by giving American audiences entertainment. Thomas preferred not to write for those "anxious to laugh and forget," but for those "grim people to whom life is real."[8] Throughout his career, though, Thomas had to write plays for star actors and actresses, even for whole casts. He wrote a part for Nat Goodwin in *In Mizzoura* and for Maurice Barrymore in *Alabama, Colonel Carter of Cartersville,* and *New Blood.* When *Alabama* extended beyond a one-act playlet for the intended cast of J. H. Stoddart, Agnes Miller, and Edward Bell, Thomas had to conceive enough characters to be acted by Palmer's entire company. To make a living as a playwright, he was forced to pay heed to dramatic fashions and to alternate serious plays with farcical ones, and quiet plays with theatrical ones. The quality of his work is thus decidedly uneven. As was the fashion, he dramatized novels, such as *Colonel Carter of Cartersville, The Jucklins, The Soldiers of Fortune,* and *The Battle Cry.* At the request of managers, he tried to capitalize on the popularity of the southern play, largely prompted by the success of *Alabama.* Palmer's refusal to produce *A Constitutional Point* in 1890 helped persuade Thomas to delay serious, explicit, and extended treatment of psychic subjects until the production of *The Witching Hour* in 1907. The critical and public excoriation of *Reckless Temple* for its social commentary and *New Blood* and *The Capitol* for their hard look at socioeconomic and political problems prompted Thomas to turn to rewrites for the stage, like *Chimmie Fadden, The Jucklins,* and *The Bonnie Brier Bush.* After the failure of *Colorado,* he wrote a series of highly successful farces that did not make his audience think. After the failure of the theme plays *The Model* and *Indian Summer,* he collaborated on or adapted the novels of others until writing *Rio Grande* and *The Copperhead.* This carpentry on the plays and novels of others, which Thomas occasionally turned to in order to make a living, nearly always gives evidence of his master craftsmanship, but rarely displays the candor or the depth of thought in his plays of the American soil. More important, they did not advance the American drama.

From a bird's-eye view of the 1891–1911 transition in American drama, however, it is not Thomas's adaptation to the commercial theater that is so unexpected but rather his often fierce independence while meeting its demands. Stranded in St. Louis after the second Dickson Sketch Club tour with no prospect for the New York production of *The Burglar,* he refused to rewrite the play so that noted actor E. H. Sothern would be in each act. For Nat Goodwin, who had commissioned a play, Thomas wrote a bas-relief part not to display the star's talents but to fit the action of *In Mizzoura.* At a time when foreign imitations and adaptations crowded the American stage, Thomas wrote thoroughly American plays. For audiences that wanted to be entertained, he wrote *Alabama* and political, socioeconomic, and psychological theme dramas.

Erosion of a Reputation

Excluding adaptations or revisions of foreign plays or novels, thirty-five of Thomas's plays opened on the New York stage from 1889 through 1911. In 1903 a theater critic estimated that scarcely a week in the last twelve years had passed when a Thomas play was not being performed somewhere in the United States;[9] and in 1909, Van Wyck Brooks surmised that "half the people in the United States who have ever seen a play at all have seen" a Thomas play.[10] After the death of Bronson Howard in 1908, Thomas was generally regarded as the dean of American playwrights. Realizing he was at the peak of his accomplishments in 1911, when *As a Man Thinks* was produced to great critical and popular acclaim, Thomas went abroad for a two-week study of the drama in England and Paris. He never returned to his former status as a playwright, however. Four of his six plays written from 1912 through 1914 had a combined total run of fifty-six nights. During the rest of his career, only *The Copperhead* was a notable triumph, and only *The Cricket of Palmy Days* had a moderate success.

With the dissolution early in the twentieth century of faith in progress, strict moral standards, and knowable standards of nature, Thomas, after 1911, found himself in an alien world, as did Henry James and William Dean Howells. New forces were taking hold of the theater. Thomas could view the expressionism of *Dr. Caligari's Cabinet* only as a cheat and could not tolerate what seemed to him to be morbidity in Eugene O'Neill's plays, as he earlier could not tolerate Ibsen's "depressing" work.

With the rise of the little theater movement in America, a new generation of critics defined the new drama by criticizing the old. History has been equally unkind to Thomas's reputation. Though he was as influential in the theater of his day as O'Neill was in his time, drama historians after Arthur Hobson Quinn, Montrose Moses, and Barrett H. Clark have nearly disregarded Thomas as a forefather of modern American drama and have

ignored the bridge between American plays of the 1870s and
1880s and modern drama.

A Retrospective View

By today's standards, a number of Thomas's characters, some
of whom gave birth to movie stereotypes, seem hackneyed.
To encourage production of their plays, Thomas and his contemporaries often wrote typecast roles for ingenues, heavies, heroes,
and the like. Thomas's heroes and villains, however, often are
atypical. The villain, who may have some admirable qualities,
is never evil, but underdeveloped. His villainy may be due to
capitalism, a puritanical environment, or his social station. The
hero may be a soft-spoken sheriff who has never killed a person,
a charismatic gambler who loves fine pictures and whose good
luck at cards is due to telepathy, or a physician who heals the
mind. The hero may accept unintended responsibility for the
villain's crime. To contemporary audiences, these and other of
Thomas's characters were a breath of fresh air in a stale theater.
The characters seemed real, had everyday concerns, and in crisp
and laconic dialogue talked as people then talked.

Today Thomas's plots—with their frequent, though subdued,
physical action, love interest, potentially happy endings, and
implausibilities—may seem melodramatic. A plot summary of
The Witching Hour suggests a melodrama of violent and sensational incidents, such as a would-be murderer disarmed by the
use of hypnotism, a daring automobile escape from a manhunt,
communication between the living and the dead, and a half
million minds telepathically influencing a sequestered jury. Contemporary audiences, on the other hand, were impressed most
by Thomas's sincerity and by the depth of his inquiry.

His composition process today may seem too much controlled
by dramatic theory. He may seem too much the stage carpenter,
his play elements too dovetailed, and his effects too studied.
To Thomas's contemporaries, however, his plays seemed plot-
less, lacking in action and situations, but marvelously constructed, without a loose end. They were innovative because
plot usually was background for character setting or theme studies. When his craftsmanship fused all play elements as in *The
Witching Hour* and *As a Man Thinks,* conjured up the presence

of the dead Abraham Lincoln in *The Copperhead,* and kept the audience's attention at a high pitch in *Arizona,* his plays became technical landmarks in the development of American drama. Thomas's subject matter, sentiment, and themes today seem dated. His plays, at times, mirror too well old-fashioned love interest, the fads of the time, topical concerns, and the limitations of the age. In staging America's strengths—her principles of liberty and equal opportunity, her physical energy as a growing industrial and political giant, and the sense of limitless possibilities as a frontier was being tamed—Thomas also staged nineteenth-century complacency, sentimentality, and naive belief in standards and progress. His psychic plays seem pseudoscientific in theme, though they were based on a thorough study of then respected scientific fields. His use of melodrama to convey theme as well as entertainment was a progressive development for American drama. Though his plays mirror too well the limitations of the turn of the century, they also interpret his age and study the evolution of American character.

These contrasting historical views suggest the rapid maturing of American drama after World War I. They also suggest the progressive maturity of Thomas's plays from 1891 through 1911. Though his plays lack the universality that would lead to their effective staging today, they were instrumental in the evolution of American drama from unrefined melodrama imitating foreign plays to skillfully constructed theme plays, American in subject and technique.

Thomas and His Contemporaries

Among the progenitors of modern American drama, Bronson Howard and Clyde Fitch surpass Thomas as dramatists of fashionable society and manners; and Fitch and James Herne in *Margaret Fleming* (1891) portray stronger and more convincing women characters than does Thomas. None of his contemporaries, however, surpasses him in the portrayal of masculine men and the writing of virile plays; and no playwright before O'Neill mirrors America more frequently and broadly than Thomas. Among his contemporaries, only Clyde Fitch, with his thirty-odd original plays, matches Thomas in output. But Fitch, a university-educated easterner, lacked Thomas's familiarity with American ge-

ography and ethnic groups, and Fitch's American history plays
are more prominent for their depiction of social life than of
period. This frequent adapter of French and German plays, in
congratulating Thomas for the success of his American play
Alabama, wrote Thomas, "I cldnt [*sic*], so didn't."[11] Howard's
most national work, *Shenandoah* (1889), is conventional and
more foreign than American in manner. Gillette's *Held by the
Enemy* (1886) and *Secret Service* (1895) are primarily action plays.
Herne in his rural plays and Thomas, both influenced by William
Dean Howells, are realists of the American soil, but Thomas
is less sentimental.

As a political and socioeconomic dramatist, Thomas had no
peer in his time. His *New Blood* and *The Capitol* are serious
and well-researched studies of national problems of his time.
Howard's *Baron Rudolph* (1881), in its treatment of capital and
labor, however, is a melodrama of the old school; and *Henrietta*
(1887), which reflects business stress, is a satire. Charles Klein's
The Lion and the Mouse (1905) and Edward Sheldon's *The Boss*
(1911) are not based on firsthand knowledge. Gillette's *Electricity*
(1910), a farce, provides but slight economic criticism.

Only Herne, who was familiar with the thought of Herbert
Spencer, Charles Darwin, and George Payne, believed as
strongly as Thomas that the theater should instruct, as well as
entertain. Only his *Margaret Fleming,* influenced by Ibsen, and
perhaps Fitch's problem plays, in their seriousness and frankness
of subject matter, point more in the direction of modern drama
than did Thomas's theme plays. No plays, however, more persuaded managers to stage serious plays than did the success of
The Witching Hour and *As a Man Thinks.* Gillette's *Electricity*
and Howard's *Kate* (1906)—which Howard called in a letter
to Thomas, whom he had asked to criticize the play, the "very
best I can do, by hard and close work, after nearly twenty-
five years of effort and experience"[12]—barely approach moder-
nity.

Only Howard approached Thomas as a force in shaping theatrical policy. In master of technique, only Fitch in an occasional
play vies with Thomas. Thomas's craft, though mechanical at
times, his writing of thoroughly American plays, and his staging
of themes that made his audience think may have been necessary
subsoil for the growth of more creative geniuses like Eugene

O'Neill, whose roots went deeper and became more universal. The evolution of American drama from imitation and adaptation of foreign plays, crude melodrama, and escapist literature to well-crafted theme plays American in subject and technique was not a struggle won in a year or a decade; nor was the evolution accomplished by any single playwright. Thomas was one of several vital spans in the bridge from post–Civil War drama to post–World War I modern drama.

Notes and References

Chapter One

1. Parenthetical dates after plays, unless otherwise indicated, refer to first New York production.
2. *National Cyclopaedia of American Biography,* vol. 14 (New York: James T. White, 1892–1977), p. 127.

Chapter Two

1. "The Drama of the Occult," New York *Sun,* November 14, 1909; in the Augustus Thomas Collection at the University of North Carolina, Chapel Hill, microfilm reel 4; hereafter cited as ATC. Newspaper clippings and microfilm copy of clippings in the collection usually do not include page numbers.
2. *The Print of My Remembrance* (New York, 1922), p. 280.
3. "Personal Power," address delivered at the Carnegie Institute of Technology, Pittsburgh, Pa., April 26, 1923, p. 28; ATC.
4. "An Inquiry Concerning the Drama," *Art World* 1 (October 1916):53.
5. "How I Wrote My Greatest Play," *Delineator* 73 (February 1909); ATC, microfilm reel 4.
6. "The Stage and Its People," Philadelphia *Telegram,* October 19, 1908; ATC, microfilm reel 4.
7. *The Print of My Remembrance,* p. 280.
8. "It Was the Old Gate," *Chicago Journal,* May 23, 1891; Harvard Theatre Collection.
9. "Next Great Play on American Jew: Augustus Thomas So Declares at a Meeting for Political Education," New York *Telegraph,* May 8 or 9, 1908; ATC, microfilm reel 4.
10. "Mr. Thomas Discourses 'The Drama of Today and Tomorrow,'" Boston *Transcript,* March 1, 1912; ATC, microfilm reel 4.
11. Preface to *The Witching Hour* (New York, 1916).
12. "Next Great Play on American Jew."
13. "Augustus Thomas to the Actor," *New York Times,* March 31, 1918, sec. 4, p. 11, col. 1.
14. "The Stage and Its People."
15. "Mr. Thomas Discourses 'The Drama of Today and Tomorrow.'"

16. "Thomas as Critic," New York *Tribune,* December 8, 1909; ATC, microfilm reel 4.

17. "Augustus Thomas, Whose Drama Impends at the Illinois Theatre, Talks of the Art of Play-Building," Chicago *Record,* April 7, 1912; ATC, microfilm reel 4.

18. "An Inquiry Concerning the Drama," p. 54.

19. Ibid., p. 52.

20. *New York Times,* May 1913; ATC, microfilm reel 4.

21. "A Play to Be Seen," *New York Times,* December 5, 1909; ATC, microfilm reel 4.

22. Boston *Evening Transcript,* February 28, 1912; ATC, microfilm reel 4.

23. "A Note on 'The Copperhead,'" *New York Times,* March 24, 1918, p. 11, col. 6.

24. "A Play to Be Seen."

25. *The Harvest Moon* (New York, 1922), pp. 80–81, 86–87.

26. Preface to *The Witching Hour* (1916), p. 14.

27. "Augustus Thomas . . . Talks of the Art of Play-Building."

28. "Outline of Yale Lecture" (manuscript note); ATC.

29. "An American National Theater," *Saturday Evening Post,* December 2, 1922, p. 23.

30. "The Drama of the Occult."

31. See chapter 5 for a discussion of the formative influences on Thomas's development of his concept of the subconscious mind and a demonstration of his application of playwriting theories and techniques to *The Witching Hour, The Harvest Moon,* and *As a Man Thinks.*

Chapter Three

1. *Alabama* (Chicago, 1898), p. 107.

2. Lionel Barrymore, *We Barrymores* (Westport, Conn.: Greenwood Press, 1974), p. 52.

3. Arthur H. Quinn, *A History of the American Drama: From the Civil War to the Present Day* (New York, 1936), 1:259.

4. New York *Herald,* November 2, 1919; ATC, XXX–3–C.

Chapter Four

1. Lucy Scott Bynum in her dissertation, "The Economic and Political Ideas of Augustus Thomas," University of North Carolina, 1954, correctly assesses the importance of *New Blood* and *The Capitol* in the history of American drama and the significance of the consistency and comprehensiveness with which Thomas's plays represent American themes and subjects.

2. Letter to his son, November 9, 1910; ATC, XXXII.

3. December 12, 1924; ATC, XXX–10–M.

Chapter Six

1. Preface to *The Witching Hour* (1916), p. 5.

2. ATC, XXIX–10–Q.

3. Thomas read most, if not all, of the books written by Hyslop and Hudson, the psychical writer most influential on Thomas's thought. Hudson's books led Thomas to become interested in the experiments of James Braid, a Manchester physician who coined *hypnotism* and provided its first physiological explanation; Jean Martin Charcot, head of the Salpêtrière, the most prestigious neurological clinic in the nineteenth century; and noted French psychologist Pierre Janet. In addition to books by Hudson and Hyslop, Thomas's East Hampton library contained numerous works on psychological and psychic phenomena.

4. *The Witching Hour* (New York, 1916), p. 51; page references hereafter cited in the text.

5. ATC, XXVI–2–A, p. 32.

6. Preface to *The Witching Hour* (1916), p. 7.

7. This motif of hatred is amplified further in Lew's anger at Hardmuth for hounding every cardplayer in Louisville for the past six months and his later desire to accomplish revenge by turning in Hardmuth to the authorities, and in Hardmuth's prosecution of Clay to vent his personal hatred of Viola's rejection of his marriage proposal.

8. *The Witching Hour* (New York: Harper, 1908), p. 103. Novelization by Thomas of the play.

9. Ibid., p. 102.

10. *The Print of My Remembrance*, p. 447.

11. *The Harvest Moon* (New York, 1922), pp. 20, 31, 33, 34, 91; page references hereafter cited in the text.

12. "A Play to Be Seen," *New York Times,* December 5, 1909; ATC, microfilm reel 4.

13. New York *Telegraph,* May 9, 1908; ATC, microfilm reel 4.

14. *As a Man Thinks* (New York, 1911), p. 192; page references hereafter cited in the text.

15. "The Psychology of the Stage," *New York Times,* November 14, 1909; ATC, microfilm reel 4.

Chapter Seven

1. "A forecast written Sep— 1917 [*sic*]"; ATC, XXIX–6–H, pp. 3–4.

2. ATC, XXXI–3–A, pp. 5–32.

3. "Mr. Thomas Discourses 'The Drama of Today and Tomorrow,' " ATC, microfilm reel 4.

4. Cincinnati *Commercial*, March 31, 1912; ATC, microfilm reel 4.

5. St. Louis *Post-Dispatch*, 1891, XXXI–3–A, p. 54.

6. *New York Times* and *World*, September 11, 1900; ATC, XXX–2–A, pp. 14–17.

7. Caspar Harold Nannes, *Politics in the American Drama* (Washington, D.C., 1960), p. 223.

8. "A forecast written Sep— 1917 [*sic*]," p. 2.

9. "About the Author," *Manhattan Theatre*, May 25, 1903; ATC, microfilm reel 4.

10. "Augustus Thomas," *World's Work* 18 (August 1909):11882.

11. ATC, XXXI–2–A, p. 61.

12. Ibid., p. 62.

Selected Bibliography

PRIMARY SOURCES

Parenthetical dates after plays, unless otherwise indicated, refer to first New York production; dates not enclosed in parentheses refer to a play's publication date. For plays with several versions, the title of only the final version is listed. Collaborations and adaptations of novels and foreign plays are indicated.

I. Dramatic Works

A. Plays for which there are manuscripts at the Augustus Thomas Collection at the University of North Carolina at Chapel Hill

1. Plays performed on the professional stage
Afterthoughts (1890).
Alabama (1891). Chicago: Dramatic Publishing Co., 1898.
Arizona (1899). Chicago: Dramatic Publishing Co., 1898; New York: Samuel French, c. 1899 and 1926; New York: R. H. Russell, 1902.
As a Man Thinks (1911). New York: Duffield, 1911; Samuel French's Standard Library, New York: French, 1911; in George P. Baker, *Modern American Plays,* New York: Harcourt, Brace, and Howe, 1921.
At Bay (1913). A collaboration with George Scarborough.
The Battle Cry (1914). An adaptation of Charles Neville Buck's novel of the same name.
The Blue Devil (Baltimore, 1920).
The Bonnie Brier Bush (c. 1897). A revision of James MacArthur's dramatization of Ian Maclaren's novel of the same name.
The Burglar (1889).
The Capitol (1895).
Champagne Charlie (1901).
Chimmie Fadden (1896).

Colonel Carter of Cartersville (1892). Adaptation of Francis Hopkinson Smith's novel of the same name.

Colonel George of Mount Vernon (Boston, 1898). New York: Samuel French, 1931.

Colorado (1901).

The Copperhead (1918). An adaptation of Frederic Landis's novel *The Glory of His Country.* New York: Samuel French, 1922; in Helen L. Cohen, ed., *Longer Plays by Modern Authors,* New York: Harcourt Brace, 1922.

The Cricket of Palmy Days (1919). New York: Samuel French, 1929.

DeLancey (1905).

Editha's Burglar (St. Louis, 1883). Based on Frances Hodgson Burnett's short story of the same name. A collaboration with Edgar Smith. New York: Samuel French, 1932.

The Earl of Pawtucket (1903). New York: Samuel French, 1917.

The Education of Mr. Pipp (1905). A dramatization of pictures by Charles Dana Gibson.

The Embassy Ball (1906).

The Harvest Moon (1909). New York: Samuel French, 1922.

The Holly Tree Inn (1892). Based on Charles Dickens's story of the same name.

The Hoosier Doctor (1898).

In Mizzoura (1893). New York: Samuel French, 1916; in Montrose Moses, ed., *Representative Plays by American Dramatists,* New York: E. P. Dutton, 1921 and 1948.

Indian Summer (1913). New York: Rosenfield, 1913.

The Jucklins (Philadelphia, 1897). An adaptation of Opie Read's novel of the same name.

A Leaf from the Woods (St. Louis, 1883).

A Man of the World (St. Louis, 1883).

The Man Upstairs (1895). New York: Samuel French, c. 1924; in *One-Act Plays for Stage and Study,* New York: Samuel French, c. 1924.

The Matinee Idol (1909). An adaptation of William Bayle Bernard's *His Last Legs.*

The Meddler (1898).

The Member from Ozark (Detroit, 1910).

Mere Man (1912).

The Model (1912).

Mrs. Leffingwell's Boots (1905). New York: Samuel French, 1916.

Nemesis (1921).

New Blood (1894).
A New Year's Call (St. Louis, 1883).
Oliver Goldsmith (1900). New York: Samuel French, 1916.
On the Quiet (1901).
The Other Girl (1903). New York: Samuel French, 1917.
A Proper Impropriety (1893). New York: Samuel French, c. 1932.
The Ranger (1907).
Reckless Temple (1890).
Rio Grande (1916).
Soldiers of Fortune (1902). An adaptation of Richard Harding Davis's play based on his novel of the same name.
The Soul Machine (1915).
Still Waters (1926). New York: Samuel French, 1926.
A Studio Picture (St. Louis, 1883).
Surrender (1892).
That Overcoat (1898).
The Witching Hour (1907). New York: Harper & Brothers, 1908; New York: Samuel French, 1916; in Arthur Hobson Quinn, *Representative American Plays,* New York: Century, 1917; in Montrose J. Moses, *Representative American Dramas National and Local,* Boston: Little, Brown, 1926.
A Woman of the World (1890).

2. Plays performed only at the Lambs Club
The Appreciator (1912).
A Constitutional Point (1905). An early version of act 2 of *The Witching Hour.* New York: Samuel French, 1932.
The King and the Footpad (1901).
The Masqueraders (1895).
The Music Box (1894).
Nellie (1912).
The Spinner (1911).

3. Motion picture scenarios
Fate Sits Weaving.
The Nightingale (1914).
Trail of the Serpent.

4. Unperformed plays
At Liberty.
The Baron. A collaboration with Martha Morton.

The Boar's Head Inn. Possibly performed at the Lambs Club.
By-Law No. 5.
A Dress Suit. Possibly performed at the Lambs Club.
Georgie Porgie.
Love Will Find the Way.
The Mule Shoe.
The Northwest.
Pittsburgh.
The Racing Sketch. Possibly performed at the Lambs Club.
The Roman Coin. Possibly performed at the Lambs Club.
A Social Fiction.
Song of the Dragon. An adaptation of John Traintor Foote's short story of the same name.
The Spider's Web. A revision of a play by Rachel Crothers and Rafael Sabatini.
The Vanishing Lady. A collaboration with Frederic Landis.

B. Plays for which there are no manuscripts in the Augustus Thomas Collection at the University of North Carolina at Chapel Hill

Alone (1875).
The Big Rise (1882).
Combustion (1884). A collaboration with Edgar Smith.
The Correspondent.
For Money (1892). A collaboration with Clay M. Greene.
A Night's Frolic (1891). An adaptation from the German.
Poor Girls (1894). An adaptation from the German.
Sue (1896). A revision of Bret Harte and T. Edgar Pemberton's *Sue.*
Three Days Out (1897).
Three of Hearts (1913). A collaboration with Martha Morton based on Harold MacGrath's story "Hearts and Masks."

II. Nondramatic Works
"An American National Theater." *Saturday Evening Post,* December 2, 1922, pp. 23, 70, 74.
"Augustus Thomas." *Current Opinion* 64 (1918):183–84.
"Augustus Thomas: Playwright. By Himself." *Outlook* 94 (January 22, 1910):212–14.
"Augustus Thomas to the Actor." *New York Times,* March 31, 1918, sec. 4, p. 11, col. 1.
Commemorative Tributes to Francis Hopkinson Smith, no. 29. New York: American Academy of Arts and Letters, 1922, pp. 1–9.

"How I Wrote My Greatest Play." *Delineator* 73 (February 1909):221–22. About *The Witching Hour.*

"An Inquiry Concerning the Drama." *Art World* 1 (October 1916): 52–55.

"The Institute's Greetings to Russia." *Art World* 2 (June 1917):255–56.

Introduction to *The Autobiography of a Play* by Bronson Howard. New York: Printed for the Dramatic Museum of Columbia University, 1914, pp. 1–6.

"Moliere, Actor and Man." *Mentor* 10 (May 1922):9–12.

"Not the Destination—But the Route." *Art World* 10 (November 1918):29–31.

"A Note on 'The Copperhead.' " *New York Times,* March 24, 1918, p. 11, col. 6.

"A Passion Play in America." *Proceedings of the American Academy of Arts and Letters and of the National Institute of Arts and Letters* 1, no. 6 (June 1, 1913):7–12.

"A Playwright's Views." *Review of Reviews* 75 (April 1927):402.

Preface to *One Act Plays for Stage and Study.* First Series. New York: Samuel French, 1925, pp. 7–9.

Prefaces to the following plays published by Samuel French (see play entries for bibliographical data): *Colonel George of Mount Vernon, The Copperhead, The Cricket of Palmy Days, The Earl of Pawtucket, The Harvest Moon, In Mizzoura, Mrs. Leffingwell's Boots, Oliver Goldsmith, The Other Girl, Still Waters,* and *The Witching Hour.*

The Print of My Remembrance. New York: Charles Scribner's Sons, 1922. Thomas's autobiography.

"Recollections of Frederic Remington," *Century* 86 (July 1913):354–61.

The Witching Hour. New York: Harper & Bros., 1908. A novel.

THE AUGUSTUS THOMAS COLLECTION
(PRIMARY AND SECONDARY SOURCES)

The Augustus Thomas Collection at the Wilson Library of the University of North Carolina at Chapel Hill is a must for a thorough study of Augustus Thomas as a dramatist, theatrical leader, and person. The collection, gathered primarily by Professor James O. Bailey from Thomas's son and wife, includes manuscripts, scrapbooks, letters, and numerous miscellaneous items. For a full listing of the items in the collection, see Jim Gayle Lewis, "An Annotated Calendar of the Augustus Thomas Collection in the University of North Carolina Library," thesis, University of North Carolina, Chapel Hill, 1969.

Elliott, Glory Thomas. "Diary and Journal of Glory Thomas Elliott," Box 33. The honeymoon diary of Thomas's daughter. Of value because of the foreword by Thomas's grandson William Elliott, which includes important biographical notes about the family. Newspaper reviews of Thomas's plays in five scrapbooks. Boxes 31 and 32. Numerous reviews cover Thomas's dramatic involvement from the mid-1880s, when Thomas organized the Dickson Sketch Club, through the production of *The Witching Hour* (1907). Essential for an understanding of contemporary critical reaction to Thomas's plays and helpful for an understanding of the development of American drama near the turn of the twentieth century.

Thomas, Augustus. Addresses. Box 29. Numerous unpublished speeches by Thomas reveal his wit as a speaker and his dramatic, political, and psychological theories.

————. Letters. Box 33. About 350 letters to his son during Luke's college years (1910–14). Provides nearly a daily account of the activities of the Thomas family during school terms and frequently mentions Thomas's dramatic and political activities.

————. Manuscript essays and notes. Box 29. A list of his more important essays and notes on the state of contemporary American drama, playwriting techniques, and the subconscious mind follows:

"Censorship." February 21, 1925. 2–K.
"George Polti, *Thirty-Six Dramatic Situations.*" 12–E.
"Get acquainted . . ." 13–H.
"I shall not attempt to review . . ." 2–D.
"I used to feel considerable pride . . ." 2–E.
"In this dossier I want to collect . . ." May 1922. 6–I.
"Much has been written . . ." 6–M.
"Notes." 13–B.
"One considerable difference . . ." 6–T.
"Outline of Yale Lecture." 2–Z.
"Props." 6–R.
" 'Seems? Nay, 'tis. I know not "seems." ' " 6–P.
"To pay my bills . . ." 6–H.
"To Write a Play." 13–A.

————. Plays. Contains one or more versions of nearly all the plays (152 versions in all).

Thomas, Lisle Colby. "A Well-Known Playwright's Wife." XXI–4–A. Three parts. The autobiography of Thomas's wife, not always consistent with Thomas's autobiography, *The Print of My Remem-*

brance. Of value because of a chronology and foreword by Thomas's grandson William Elliott, which provides genealogical and biographical information about the family.

OTHER SECONDARY SOURCES

I. Bibliographies

Baker, Blanch M. *Theatre and Allied Arts: A Guide to Books Dealing with the History, Criticism, and Technic of the Drama and Theatre and Related Arts and Crafts.* 1952. Reprint. New York: Bloom, 1967. An excellent annotated bibliography of about six thousand volumes on drama and the theater published between 1885 and 1948.

Meserve, Walter J., ed. *American Drama to 1900: A Guide to Information Sources.* Detroit: Gale Research, 1980. An essential annotated bibliography of American drama, but not the American theater. Covers drama history, criticism, and playwrights.

II. Biography, Criticism, and Other Reference Sources

Bergman, Herbert. "Augustus Thomas: Dramatist of His Age." Ph.D. diss., University of Wisconsin, 1952. Compares Thomas's comedies and major theme and regional plays with dramas by Clyde Fitch and David Belasco. Based on detailed research; good bibliography.

Bernheim, Alfred L., et al. *The Business of the Theatre: An Economic History of the American Theatre, 1750–1932.* Well researched and documented; valuable for an understanding of the commercial theater for which Thomas wrote.

Boucicault, Dion. "The Future of American Drama." *Arena* 12 (November 1890):641–52. Calls for a "new drama concerned with social and scientific problems, such as 'the great struggle between labor and capital' " four years before the production of *New Blood,* Thomas's theme play on socioeconomics.

Brooks, Van Wyck. "Augustus Thomas." *World's Work* 18 (August 1909):11882–85. Estimates that in 1909 half the people in the United States who had ever seen a play had seen one of Thomas's plays.

Bynum, Lucy S. "The Economic and Political Ideas of Augustus Thomas." Ph.D diss., University of North Carolina, 1954. A mature assessment of Thomas's political and economic plays and their thoroughly American nature.

Coad, Oral Sumner, and Edwin Mims, Jr. *The American Stage.* The Pageant of America Series, vol. 14. New Haven, Conn.: Yale University Press, 1929. A history of the American stage through Gordon Craig. Recognizes that *New Blood* and *The Capitol* are significant studies of economics and politics and that Thomas is perhaps America's most representative playwright through 1911.

Davenport, W. A. "Augustus Thomas—From 'Mizzoura.'" *World's Work* 46 (May 1923):78–83. Interviews Thomas as the executive chairman of the Producing Managers' Association. Indicates Thomas's concerns as producing chairman and provides a biographical sketch.

De Wagstaffe, William. "Perpetuating Charles Frohman's Work." *Theatre Magazine* 22 (September 1915):117–18, 142. Includes some of Thomas's views about American drama and theater and his theatrical plans as art director of the reorganized Frohman Company.

Hartman, John Geoffrey. *The Development of American Social Comedy from 1787 to 1936.* 1939. Reprint. New York: Octagon Books, 1971. A survey of American social comedy as reflecting contemporary manners, customs, and thought. Contains a brief discussion of *The Earl of Pawtucket* as representing the international contrast and *Mrs. Leffingwell's Boots* as mirroring conflict between the individual and society.

Herron, Ima Honaker. *The Small Town in American Drama.* Dallas: Southern Methodist University Press, 1969. *Arizona, In Mizzoura,* and *The Copperhead,* and about three hundred other plays (including relatively unknown ones) discussed as mirroring village and small-town life.

Hewitt, Barnard. *Theatre U.S.A. 1668–1957.* New York: McGraw-Hill, 1959. Includes Heywood Broun's review for the New York *Tribune* of *The Copperhead.*

Howells, William Dean. "The Recent Dramatic Season." *North American Review* 122 (March 1901):468–70. A contemporary analysis of the New York production of *Arizona,* one of seven or eight plays of New York's dramatic season of 1900–1901, according to Howells, which refutes the charge that the American theater is in decay. Calls *Arizona* American in atmosphere, charming in the "intense distinctness" of its local color, "extraordinarily vivid" in the picturesqueness of life of the Southwest, and sharp and rapid in action.

Hudson, Thomas Jay. *The Law of Psychic Phenomena.* Chicago: A. C. McClurg, 1893. The psychical writer most influential on Thomas's thought; led Thomas to become interested in the experiments of James Braid, who coined *hypnotism* and provided its first physiological explanation; Jean Martin Charcot, head of the most prestigious neurological clinic in the nineteenth century; and noted French psychologist Pierre Janet.

Hughes, Glen. *A History of the American Theatre, 1700–1950.* New York: Samuel French, 1951. Little commentary on Thomas, but for American drama from 1870–1900 has chapters on managers and old stars, new stars and dramatists, and forms and phenomena, as well as a chapter on American drama from 1900–1910.

Meserve, Walter J. *An Outline History of American Drama.* Totowa, N.J.: Littlefield, Adama, 1965. Sketches trends in American drama; includes numerous plot summaries but little critical assessment.

Moody, Richard. *America Takes the Stage: Romanticism in American Drama and Theatre, 1750–1900.* Bloomington: Indiana University Press, 1955. Mentions only Thomas's *Alabama, In Mizzoura,* and *The Copperhead;* a solid study of native themes and characters in American drama as they embody the romantic spirit.

Moses, Montrose J. *The American Dramatist.* 1911. Revised edition. 1925. Reprint. New York: Blom, 1964. A basic history of American drama covering major dramatists, including Thomas, and native dramatic forms.

―――. "The Drama, 1860–1918." In *The Cambridge History of American Literature.* Edited by William P. Trent et al. New York: Macmillan, 1933. 3:266–98. An important survey; notes Thomas's skilled craftsmanship and the relative independence of his theme plays from the demands of the commercial theater.

Nannes, Caspar Harold. *Politics in the American Drama.* Washington, D.C.: Catholic University of America Press, 1960. Study of American plays with political themes performed on the Broadway stage from the 1890s through 1959. Of limited value.

Nathan, George J. "In Memoriam." *American Mercury* 8 (May 1926):117–20. A scathing attack on Thomas as a dramatist by a critic of the "new drama" that arose after 1911.

New York Times Theatre Reviews, 1870–1919. 5 vols. and 1 vol. index. Salem, N.H.: Arno, 1976. Essential for a study of American drama before Eugene O'Neill.

Notables in the American Theatre. Edited by Raymond D. McGill. Clifton, N.J.: James T. White, 1976. Includes an index by title of New York productions from 1900 to the 1970s, with the name of the theater at which the play was performed, the date of opening, and number of performances.

Odell, George C. D. *Annals of the New York Stage.* 15 vols. New York:

Columbia, 1924–49. A detailed chronicle of the New York theater through 1894.

Quinn, Arthur Hobson. *A History of the American Drama: From the Civil War to the Present Day.* New York: F. S. Crofts, 1936. Best and most comprehensive survey and critical assessment of Thomas's plays and contributions to the American drama and of the 1860–1911 period in American drama. Includes a list of all significant plays from 1860 to 1936, with dates of publication and first performance.

Salem, James M. *A Guide to Critical Reviews: Part 1: American Drama, 1909–69.* 2d ed. Methuen, N.J.: Scarecrow Press, 1973. Lists reviews of *Arizona, As a Man Thinks, The Copperhead, The Harvest Moon, Indian Summer, Mere Man, The Model, Nemesis, Palmy Days, Rio Grande,* and *Still Waters.*

Sievers, W. David. *Freud on Broadway: A History of Psychoanalysis and the American Drama.* New York: Hermitage House, 1955. Traces the influence of psychoanalysis on Broadway plays by Americans from Thomas through Arthur Miller and William Inge.

Wilson, Graff B. *Three Hundred Years of American Drama and Theatre.* Englewood Cliffs, N.J.: Prentice-Hall, 1973. Surveys the history of drama and theater, recognizing that Thomas made "substantial" contributions to American playwriting and was influential in abolishing the belief that native themes or subject matter was not attractive to the public.

Winter, William. *The Wallet of Time, Containing Personal, Biographical, and Critical Reminiscence of the American Theatre.* 1913. Reprint. Freeport, N.Y.: Books for Libraries Press, 1969, 2:529–57. Important reminiscences by a contemporary reviewer of *Alabama, Colonel Carter of Cartersville, Oliver Goldsmith, The Witching Hour* ("a great play"), and *As a Man Thinks.*

Index

DATE DUE
REMINDER

**Please do not remove
this date due slip.**